HUNGER

HUNGER

MAIA SPRING CARABAJAL

༞

RUBEDO
2022

Hunger
Maia Spring Carabajal

Published in 2022 by
RUBEDO PRESS
Auckland, New Zealand

ISBN: 978-0-9951245-4-7

© Maia Spring Carabajal 2018
Maia Spring Carabajal asserts the moral right
to be identified as the author of this work.

All rights reserved.
No part of this work may be reproduced
without express permission from the publisher.
Brief passages may be cited by way of criticism,
scholarship, or review, as long as full
acknowledgment is given.

Cover concept
by Maia Spring Carabajal
Design and Typography
by Aaron Cheak

WWW.RUBEDO.PRESS

CONTENTS

1. Venus in Gemini, 1

2. Mars in Cancer, 17

3. Jupiter in Leo, 35

4. Mercury in Aries, 97

5. Venus in the Seventh, 185

6. Mars in the Eighth, 261

7. Sagittarius Rising, 285

For Cody Clark
(1988–2021)

This is madness
but a kind of hunger.
What good are my questions
in this hierarchy of death
where the earth and the stones go
Dinn! Dinn! Dinn!

ANNE SEXTON

Hunger

1. *Venus in Gemini*

08102009

I MISS YOU,
two hundred and seventy-eight times,
I counted, in the morning.

I love you,
a lot like things are beautiful,
how?

08172009

HIS TONE BECOMES COARSE.
The sugar spills over the floor.
No one reaches for the broom.

If she can't recall their sweetness on her tongue
she would like the reminder
of where it's gone ...
grain between her bare feet and the tile.
Sliding about with a taught mouth.

There is one thing left to do.
She ponders how the taste
is so easily misplaced.
Like the sand in her bed,
best in limited amounts.

If she hadn't discarded
of all that sweet ...
into the dustpan, off to the trash can ...
there would be dunes,
dunes of spilt sugar all in her room,
inside of her closet, next to the bed,
guarding the refrigerator door.
The motions are all custom
but she will repress them.
Like a sneeze that passes,
that will come again.

This time maybe
she will wait until the black ants invade.

08252009

I WOULDN'T WISH IT ON YOU
but it should come.
When it does
you will do what you can.

You could take from it.

It will come down hard.
In that moment you will find
a place to hide your head.
Or you could dance,
you could open your tongue
to the gray sky and drink

breathe the wet of storms
passed and promised,
through every pore in your
nostrils and cheeks.

I would try not to present
you with so many possibilities.
They come and go on their own,
cyclical, abundant;
take it in when you can
ring it out,
get it back again.

Please, so I could stand
across the intersection
and observe you dripping.

The excess traveling your form,
downward from the crown of your head,
off your shivering shoulders.

08302009

THE ORGANS ALIGN THEMSELVES
upright we step forward
into each other's space.
The hard wall
spoken with posture.

Poised so our mouths loosen
lips revolve,
spun and bitten
licked, warm
and pull forward with cheeks high
near the deep purple under the eyes.

Slow motion
the first sound of the ocean
at any time of day.
The startling power that grows
rhythmic.
You are in its belly
treading her great mysterious stomach.

Returning to shore, uncertain
and exhausted.
Pounded in an exhilarating struggle
leaving you breathing hard on your back in sand.
Precious as meditative breaths.
Gasping in gratitude.
In that rest
feeling the balance of
freedom and captivity.
Elaborate palace

made of flesh.
Home for one moment
you find god, and are relinquished.
Settled in comforting amber
with a single embrace.

11022009

WHY IS IT EASIER TO LOVE YOU
when you are gone?
I see that big dripping moon
and it is still you.
Wherever I go, there you are
up there wetting the structure below
with that silver glow, comforting
as that late afternoon amber
you taught me to impose.

When the sun sets through my blinds
you are one of the many glittering particles
drifting in my mind.
I don't grab at yours anymore
since they have slid through my fingers
so many times.

I let you float in and out of the light,
as my eyelids become heavy
underneath the calming weight
of your memories.
I curl into a ball
as if you were holding me right there.
I am gently let down into sleep.
In the warmth of an afternoon window
I can still dream of you.

11082009

A STORY IS RECOLLECTED,
a path is folded back over upon,
so that a weary traveler turns on their bruised toes
and shifts on twisted ankle.
Small glinting strands of webbed thought
delicately bind a dry path
so that no matter how little it is tended,
moist by the wet of a spoken tongue
or wave of emotion swelling in a hopeful heart
it is eternally held.

I struggle,
left to grasp detail and vocabulary
for that overwhelming surge of energy.
The violent shine,
radiating glow of warmth.

A calloused heel strikes rough pavement
causing friction
a flame traveling upward
singeing the stubble made on my legs
lighting my weak knees
heating my thighs.

My organs
levitated by pale memories
that slip in and out
and underneath
raising my stomach into my throat,
a swift shift echoes one booming note
which startles me

and all that was suspended
is let down into a sore heap.

Habitual hope
the great lump of sweet in my throat.
Mixing acidic with the bile.
Retorts rise onto my tongue.
Organs bounce like atoms shook,
a jostled can of carbonation.

You have bruised me in the most strange
and peculiar places,
so that if I were to reach for another
he would press against my wounds
and I would moan in pain
misinterpreted.

Reflections or something

MY BROTHER IS A BEARDED SQUID THAT
lives at the center of an endless drought.
He showed me how to hold people with locked elbows.
He left careful instructions
on how to turn a lover into an inanimate object.
I did not understand his language.
I was left to evaluate gestures and movement.
In time I have come to read him fluently.
I read him with my fingertips,
running them along his cold templates.

Now he speaks in wind
that moves in pitches I do not correlate.
We are always on different planes.
I expect not to understand
what he is saying,
but keep a little hope for my old friend,
at some point the future may give me
a translation.
And he never catches a phrase in my hissing.
I receive no word as to whether
he has begun to hear any distinct meaning.

Sarcasm

IT TOOK AWHILE TO LEARN
and practice
sarcasm.
I've made a habit
of saying what
I do not mean.

Skin and bones

SKIN AND BONES GETS ANXIOUS,
starts knocking on midnight doors.
They open, but he's feeling selective.

His mind is bound in linear stripes
impressed with thermal perceptions.
He flips through their prints
and finds comfort in the images.

Proof that familiarity yields depth
that can be tapped by growing downward.

Circling mental blocks,
perpetual primitive self preservation,
becoming one with melancholy
and nostalgia.

Hinges, bravely explores,
heavy-lidded and dreamwalking,
he seems
to earn transcendence.

03232010

YOUNG MINDS ARE
tools of innovation,
fruits of evolution's labor.
Products of common knowledge,
conventional wisdom.
Grooming and pruning
the noosphere.
Pose questions,
to be shown shared reality,
the dilemma of existence's consensus.

Inspire us with corruption,
with chaos.
Reform to allow beauty to happen.

Instead of diluting the self
over and over, until one is
mild enough to the limp tongues
of dying traditions.

2. *Mars in Cancer*

05262010

I NOTICED YOU IN THE AISLE
suddenly turning
to shove both my hands
into a bowl of honey.
Looking down at them in terror
I immediately began to smear them
on my jeans.
All the while the evidence
becoming more conspicuous.

It took three rolls of paper towels
to get my hands clean.

08102010

I AM HOLLOWED TO FEEL YOU GO.
True love is also
the pain felt in its absence.

I am still feeling.
I fear going numb
and losing all passion.

I embrace the destruction
of our past reality as one.
You have exercised your freedom
and I can only stand in awe and attention
at your deliberation.
Humbled to witness something other
than your apathy.

From the death by your strong words
a slow future is birthed.
I am surprised that my infant can be reborn.
My teenage heart wrings her fingers red
under a blue sun that rises
for an eternity.

11112010

IT CAME AGAIN, THIS PHYSICAL PLACE
where my subconscious desires
all rush into the grid of open eyes.

In wakefulness
I am reminded of past relations,
future intentions.
They all manage to remain intact.

My loves stay with me in dreams.
I wake to feel separate, devastated.
And I am so attached to this existence, this life.
The pieces are woven by invisible threads
shone in illumination of meditation.
Small epiphanies grace the dawn.

I integrate the nuance,
and relocating myself within the dynamic flux:
chaotic, electric, stagnant, turning, operating
regardless of my understanding.

My will to fathom keeps me churning
sending tension into my brain
where my infinite questions pulse with
painful reminders,
until I let them free,
in a single loving breath.

Brother No. 73

REMOVE ME FROM THE SHELF AS A DUSTY GLASS.
You blow into it and get a flurry
of memories in your eyes.
Sudden annoyances light a fire
in your chest as you rub your face.
You fill me with water over the sink.
Clear liquid is not strong enough,
you reach for thick whiskey.
I hold it for you
all the same.

Your thoughts drift between sips
like cigarette smoke.
I am in your hands, once again.
I am at your lips.

I have felt it before,
I have thought it,
and I go there as well.

Your throat is warm,
the air is cold,
the night is dark,
and we see that nothing
burns as brilliantly as before.

When we want to feel calm
we burn herb.
When we want to see god
we drop acid.
When we want to feel bliss

we take molly.
There is too much shadow
to shed light.
We fear to embrace
the simplicity.
We turn our attention to the work
we must do:
solitary innovations,
the audacity to evolve
in the ever-droning cynicism
and entropy.

Evasion

I SIT HALF LOTUS ON A BLUE BENCH
chain-smoking cigarettes.
I see you stride briskly through a vast deserted space
where the buildings, stretched above the towers and
parking garages, block our views.

Your height was magnificent.
I saw your legs stretch up from the ground.
A passing plane brushed the ends of your golden crown.
I was a planet that orbited your reality,
held off by your gravity.
If I could will myself closer,
a universe would collapse upon itself.

01172011

ALLOWING THE DANCE OF ENERGIES
to bend into my selective perforated parameters.
Becoming a playful seduction
causing my heart to burst
late afternoon illuminations.
Receptions for small monuments.
My nurturer surpasses lust
taking joy in returning offerings.
Hoping we can go again and again.
Hoping we continue to seek fulfillment
in serving each other
with affectionate expressions.
Intimate display,
The silencing of duality,
in our constant ability to shift
from giver to receiver.

03012011

AT YOUR FUNERAL
I wore nothing
but the mud that covered my limbs
while digging your grave in the pouring rain.

I cried tears of joy that warmed my face,
and found *amrita*, once more,
in a fit of ecstatic laughter.

I tore a fist of hair from the crown of my head
and left it at your toes, six feet under.

I kissed the cheeks of your ghost
with a loving mouth,
before sending you off

to make room in my bed
for the future king.

03242011

FOR THE WOMAN
who has forgotten her divinity:
who lies dormant awaiting invitations of bliss.

I will remind her that her flesh
is made of sun that radiates
and conducts with gravitational force
to encompass
desire, unconditional love,
and worship.
Her organs, soft and effective
house the cosmic truth,
manifestations of every tale of creation,
form, action, emotion.
The eternal Shakti.
Every pulse of sensuality and love
is an ecstatic gift that she emanates.

( )

SORTING THINGS OUT,
creating stacks of what is mine.
Steadily building mountains
of my own impressions
Coming back to my reality.
This aloneness, comforting and full
of unuttered ideas and conversation.
Lost in a journey of mind,
let off in an antigravity of unknown.
Picking the locks of heavy doors,
flinging them wide with excited hands
to find a dark room filled with emptiness,
where no man had thought to fix a light switch.
Pupils tremble above still, open lips,
tonguing the back of my teeth
making silent friction
that cannot describe imagination's creations
in the endless possibility of that that that that ...
the longer I attempted to understand,
the more I questioned it.

04082011

COME OVER,
new friend.
I can sing
and dance
play some instrument,
read you poetry.
Come see my abnormally large
accumulation of half-read books
and mediocre record collection.
We can chain-smoke
while I say some
honest things.
I will all be entertaining,
until you start to pick at
the cat hair
blanketing the couch cushions.
You'll say something like,
I've got work early,
then you will leave and I will go
back to sorting and touching
all of my possessions,
sometimes giving into
the impulse to jot down or sing
a thought.
It will be very simple,
and you may come back around
for another show,
until I am no longer capable
of captivating you.

05032011

ONE THOUSAND TINY PARTICLES
turn over,
what can be expressed here.
I have this overwhelming feeling
of flatness.
I cannot be drawn into conversation ...
Let it go ...
the gods are telling me so.
These are our preferences.
Our choices.
Respect them.
I do so, cringing,
like a child being told "no".

Elder,
my heart sings wild symphonies
that I could not write.
In notes? In laughter?
What markings does the heart make?

I am young as before
conception of reality.
Wise as the
existence of all things.
Limited by ideology.

Unspoken philosophies.
No connection
nor design.
I have collapsed all of the functions
that bring me to their romance,

with silence.
My skin is tight and itchy.
Completely black hole.
I am drunk, high, and hallucinating
on void.
Everything inside of me is shaking strange.
I want to run but I cant,
I must stay here, and feel so vast,
so misplaced.

05042011

LET THE WORLD MAKE WAR AND CHAOS.
I am floating
somewhere in between.
My heart sweats light
as I tell my mind to quiet
what it cannot fathom or rationalize.

Pleasantly unattached
Finding I can be with peace.

Let me forget how I have come here,
for a moment
so that I can dream of a brilliance
I had not believed I could create before.
Let me sing notes
that can be lapped up,
in sips of illumination.

05052011

WHAT HAS HAPPENED TO ME?
How have I lost all romance?
Identity clings to symbols,
monuments
where flowers were placed as offerings
over and over.
I struggle to detach
from grief.

Stone pain.
I once skipped along the surface,
now I have sunken in
heavy at the bottom
below a rush of movement,
losing momentum.
It is hard and cold here,
where I am defeated.
Forgiveness is a lost song
that hums silently from a deep dream,
rooted in the tip of my spine.
I hear a distant melody that echoes
against the caverns of young memory.
Softly making consonants, scattered
and aggravating as I attempt
to designate reason.

My back is tight,
everything cramps numbly.
Stagnant, stale
death in the face of angel
who has forgotten her beauty.

Once I felt vast,
my mind split open
into infinities,
each one reflecting eternities.
I was unknown,
the universe appeared to be
the greatest myth ever told.
My skin invisible,
and everything around me
pulsed and glowed.

Now it has all come back to silence,
a reflection of the many layers
that stifle ascendance.
I see all that is broken and starving.
And so I sang
as loud and honest as I could be.
yet I found my voice,
could not reach that high sea.

These words, these tones
are the clicking selections of a lock
that I will turn
to retrieve freedom from form,
from this illusion of scarcity,
frailty and flatness.

I will sleep so lightly tonight;
feeling I have not truly lived,
again I lay down without
the company of bliss.
I dream loose metaphors,
that tell me to tirelessly seek
and rediscover love,
come morning.

3. *Jupiter in Leo*

05082011

OH, BABY DOLL,
Oh, baby doll,
here is your aching heart.
Try not to,
you won't want to,
feel these pains.

Oh sweet young thing,
Oh sweet young thing,
no man has known your inner language,
your tongues paint portraits
that cannot be shown,
and so you must be alone.

My little one,
My little one,
you're hidden in daylight,
try not to give yourself
to the night.

Oh darling girl,
you've no choice but numbness.
With skin set aflame so long
you're left in ashes.

Oh barren child,
your expressionless face
will sometimes wear a smile
in the vastness
of space.

You inanimate star.
You cosmic unobtainable.
Loveless and cynical.
Spent, dry
thing.

05092011

DON'T YOU WORRY.
I'll keep the light on
for this delicate thing.
While I sift through layers,
questioning intuition
and invisible fears.
I'm sorry,
I don't trust you.
I cannot trust myself.
because not all of this is mine,
I don't honor it.
Still, you're welcome in.
Step lightly,
be honest.
Show you your heart
because although you may not notice,
I have already given you mine.
Show me your truths,
so that there will be
nothing to deny.
I am exhausted,
but please, come inside.

05112011

GRAND EMOTION
churning underneath my heart
waiting to be wielded
into some form of action.
I clench my jaw
and wait for solitude
to let it all ring through my pen.
A bit more dull,
processed.
Hello, old strangers.
Hello, old friends.
Hello, and goodbye
to the fickle ones
who let me believe
I could depend
on them.
I am floating now
far out where the waves
let me sleep.
When the stars appear
I have found a home again.
I have no company,
nothing to defend,
in solitude.
Love
and resolution.
I revel
in meditations of unification.
Unconditional and limitless.
Pens bleed dry
under my heavy hand.

Pages fill
with realization.
What beautiful thin mirrors
made for my mind.
Here are the confines
of my lack of faith.
Bursting one million colors
on a slick dripping canvas.
I am chaos
that finds peace and complexity
with art, I will cure everything.

05292011ii

WARM YOUNG THING,
your body is on fire.
Something has bloomed
from within,
sending light from your eyes,
harmony from your throat,
and every pore of your breathing skin
exudes a glow.
As these unconscious travelers
flock to you like distracted moths,
you find they can not fathom your language,
nor the frequency you pulse.
You are unknown.
Your passion is a tongue
lost in night.
You left your body in dreamless sleep
for another fertile star.
You've adapted awkwardly.
Fumbling with words
that cannot define being.
Animal,
whose heart pumps vitality vigorously,
exposed beneath a full moon
and a blanket of galaxies.
Lonely, and untouched.

05302011

I PLANNED TO TAKE A CANDLE
and a box of matches
into his psyche
to discover and illuminate
his depth.
Raw and skinned
in the morning.
Over the sink,
over his cup of tea.

But she,
she took her tongue and parted his throat
to lap every bit of pain out,
a delicate healing art
with sensual, sweet kinesthetics.
She made warm contact
and let him feel his powerful heart,
allowing him to feel his skin again.
Her touch healing what words could not.

06012011

TIMID STARS GREET ME
dim and friendly,
I gaze up at them
wondering what I am.

An easeful water dance,
I feel a settling occur.
Remembering how
I began to lose my heart
in the sickening churn.
I release so many spoils
over the edge of this ancient vessel.
I am a wanderer,
acquainted with others
but distant,
with eyes looming over vastness.
Wondering if I'll find another
who dreams of discovering
that same island
to inhabit and co-create.

Distant hope,
a rising sun
that brilliantly illuminates.
I cannot shut my eyes
on the possibilities ...

06062011

WHAT HAS KEPT US APART FOR SO LONG?
How are we separate?
I look in from the outside of our home,
through windows of compassion and empathy.
We run into and through one another
like warm light.
What mirrors outweighs our sense of individuality.
We melt together.

06112011

DULL PAIN NUMBED BY FORCED LOGIC
where there is no visual,
where the spark of emotion is not fed
by dry embrace,
I must accept that the memories
no longer exist.
They have gone frail
and whisper faint outlines
from the depths of my mind.
In dark shelves pages yellow,
like ancient romance
written with ink of
infinite wells and salt water.
The thought and feeling
of knowing your every nuance
produced a skeleton key
given in waking dream.
The symbol does not fit into the lock.
Intentions, creations
ideals scrawled
pressing novels of potential,
encoding intricate feeling,
re-writing the cells
that make me physical.
I fell asleep with him inside of me
and in a dream, he planted a seed
that began to bud.
Enamored by its absurdity
I fed the new thing,
nurtured it and began to call it my own.
It bore fruit

that I mistakenly consumed.
It bore fruits
that consumed me.
I could have retreated,
shaken it all loose,
but the messages slipped in deeply
and festered inside of me.
I call on witches
making appointment to designate.
Asking them desperately
to release the laws
that I unconsciously abided.
I ask them to set fire to the records,
and leave me with only
the texts written
by my own hand.

06112011ii

HE PLACED ANCHORS ON MY ANKLES
and waist
I was dropped down into the bay
off a city dock.
Waiting in a metaphor
to be released by anyone who cared
to find and free me.

06152011

I WOULD NOT SAY
the dark words
I repeat to myself
to you.
I would not limit you.
We speak to ourselves
like militant gridmen,
still our greater pieces
remain free.
That expanse
of metaphor and emotion,
calling to us
in sleep
and in day trance.
Like remembering the act of breath.
We are forever in movement.
Sea and stars,
burnt out and born again.
I will not hold you in my mind,
I will let you out and into transformation
observing from a distance
as you shed another identity to reform,
realign, re-mend with an ever more
transparent skin.
When you have entered your forest
and taken so many turns,
I will let your impressions run through my spine,
heart, and in my minds eye—
feeling and knowing that you have become
new again.
When I see you once more;

when you allow me an embrace,
I will silently feel out the places of pain
seeking release,
the knots in your shoulders
going soft.
The pressure behind your forehead
ceases to stop up your imaginations.
I will delight in the potential of your
new creations.
Gorgeously ascending,
you are the light human
born again from the womb of a far-off fertile star.
I love you,
friend.

06152011ii

BEAUTY SINGS INFINITIES
in every cell and atom,
humming vibrantly.
Joyous harmony.
Buzzing through my veins.
Overflowing gratitude.
Thank you. Thank you. Thank you.
I love you. I love you. I love you.
I love you. I love you.

06202011

ALIGNMENT
with empowerment
sends me off into
infinite fits
convinced that my attempts and
exhaustion of energies
will steer a river.
Leaking, limped.
Starved, frail.
Discovering error,
a misplaced faith.
Minuscule inconsistencies
summoning catastrophe.

07012011

DESIRE, DESIRE:
makes me cramp,
leaves me numb, mute,
and immobile.
Silent longing.
Enters infatuation.
Enters obsession.
A wild sea
that I fall asleep inside of
and dream I am the moon.
Above the fat clouds.
Above the heavy rain.
Above the angry turning
waters that drown me.
They took the siren's tones
from my throat
and pumped it with salt.
Filled me up with foam
and offered me to the sea's inhabitants.
I did not know peace
until being twisted.
I had no song until
I had forgotten form.
I did not know
what you were
until I was gone.

07132011

WAIT.
Don't go.
I still want you here.
You are my friend.
Thank you for checking in.
I wish you would stay longer.

I still want someone to argue
about philosophy with.
I want someone around
who knows my soul.
I want my male counterpart.
You know the spectrum of my voice,
you know the landscape of my mind,
the harmonies of my heart.
Colorado is beautiful.
I will paint you a piece
of the rolling hills in my chest
to remind you that this is
a vast destination as well.
I wanted to make music
that would enter their souls
and realign their spines
with you.
We could change the world
with our convergence.
Don't go. Don't go.

You taught me
that I can have spirits live inside of me,
without using them as a weapon against myself.

You have a home,
nestled in every organ
of my body,
a palace in my psyche.
Your name and face is clear
in my vision of unity.
Please don't leave.
I am not ready to be alone yet.

07242011

THERE WERE PIECES OF GRAY MATTER THAT HELD
past experience.
They buzzed when air was breathed into their lungs.
Familiar wind breezed through chimes that rung familiar notes.
Phrases, riffs,
that took the gut.
Notes that introduce buried memories
hidden under currents by restraint.
Attempts at self mastery
proven insignificant to passions.
What the heart desires
it forever resonates with.
What the mind perceives
it will not forget.
Go on,
strangle the cords,
take your lessons,
earn your wisdom,
and choke the subtle exchange
with the knot you tie with your tongue.
Pull tight and the umbilical tears.
You are reborn.
Still
the psyche takes forbidden
pleasure in the past.
Sometimes
we live in that.
I go back so many times.
I go back to the visual
of my toes hanging over the edge of a dock.

I was six years old gazing into still water
when I found loneliness for the first time.
I put my hands right on it.
Gave it a name and
shed a tear into the lake.
I buried you shallow
and sometimes go back
to pull the earth from your face
and contemplate the pupils
behind your pale eyelids.
Once we danced stiff over graves.
Those nights I am not in my room.
I am not with a lover, I am not with a friend
I am gone in trance,
in a lucid viewing of our past.
I am there, and I feel my heart sing.
I feel my spine pulsing.
I smell the home in your skin.
I see the shape of your shoulders and hips
and yes, I place my hands on them.
I hold you still with your heart beating in my palms
I kiss the flesh of your cheeks.
I taste the way your mouth is.
Fantasies tell my present that
I do not honor it.
They say to my future that
there will be pain like this again.
The cord slips back into place
and I am a fool.
I am the fool who dishonors
the new reality I have created.
I am the fool
who loses the power in detached observation
by sinking into the past.

09232011

IN THE EVENT OF A MAJOR CATASTROPHE
try to find me
because you're the type of person
that I'll be looking for.

11272011

I WILL EMBRACE
the familiar connection
that fills me with so much bliss.
I crave it.
I slow the momentum
of my need for warmth
with logic and assessment of inconsistency.
I am the constant observer,
in tune
but unattached.
It is infinitely moving
like water,
like every simple conscious cell
is forever turning
to express itself.
I accept chaos
with unflinching presence.
I will be with these emotions,
this passion,
this hide and seek.
For I have caught a glimmer
of hope, in the crack of a barrier
that guards my desire.
This hope does not wither in fear's shadow.
It wants the fulfillment
of an open heart.
I remain with uncertainty
and pangs of fear
that ask me to retreat.
I press further
on this sweet patch of soft pleasure.

Letting it give without bruising.
I had observed it bitter and green,
and now take delight in the change of season.
Watching as a living thing
becomes comprehensible
as it ripens.
A thing that may be offered
to the mother
but not before I have attempted
to catch it in my mouth.

01001010001010011

I FELT A LOOSE FANTASY AND ASSUMED I HAD
made it alone.
It drifted through the atmosphere of my living room by
the turn of an overhead fan.
Small dusts and old skins entered my lungs unseen.
I felt it coarse through my veins as it gave life to my
heart.
I watched my skin glow in the reflection of another pair
of eyes.
I felt a loose fantasy swallow my psyche
with a wide transparent mouth.
I was welcomed into the great gut of ecstatic systems
to be processed and reorganized.

Boom tea

HOW ARE YOU?
Come on in.
This is how we have been doing it,
by the fridge, next to the stove.
This is how we are.
This is how we have been.

We have been doing it all the entire time.
Right here
while you were gone.
Now you have come back.
We would like to tell you
well,
it's all here,
it's all fine,
it's all happening
right now.
It always has been.

Brother No. 89

BROTHER
here is our vast churning mother
who nurtures so many living mysteries.
She breathes in their unified rhythm
and forever invites us back home
to her womb
where we float and flow
in her embryonic fluid
like the new infants that we become
before we have clothed ourselves
and after we have forgotten our wisdom.

This the bed of ancient sea shells
with consciousness all dried out,
glowing warm
and incubating our salt skin
reflecting that great sun,
the father,
we could never place our hands upon
but still thrive on his distant power.
Here we breathe
with our tummies in time with the tide.

Here are the rich green leaves
of the elder tree.
These are the veins
pumping water through and through
as they inhale our charging exhalation.
Here is their hard neck and arms
his waist, her hips,
and the many red fingers

that hold the dark dank earth
from below
with dirt-caked nails.
Here is a handful of soft soil
it smells like birth.
It tastes like your lover's mouth
and sweat.
Here you are
with the sun on your closed lids
and the earth under your bare feet.
You feel how you and all thriving
are sustained by the same things.
You forget that you are not the tree.
You take water from the pores of your shins.
You draw light from the crown of your head.
You bear fruit for the fox,
the sparrow, and the children.

I forget too.
I remember that I am the tree.
I remember that I am also you.

Here, here is my hand.
It is ours. It always has been.
Here is my vast empty space
that I welcome you into.
Here, here is my unconditional, infinite
love and belief in you.

Here is my ever-expanding gratitude
thank you, thank you.

Checking in

I AM DIGESTED
and flushed down the vortex
to remember
that I am not mine.
Shadows come in Pisces.
I am more like water.
More likely to misplace pieces of myself
in darkness.
My dreams become secrets
in heavy sleep.
Awareness plays hide and seek
and refuses to receive
the root of my condition.
Last month I wrote poems of peace.
Today, I teeter
on the thin line between ether and burial.
Treading water reminds me of my limbs.

I hear a layer of harmonies
like locusts.
I feel heat and hear it say
that I cannot fathom its light.
I take the one taste.
I try to store the invisible symphony
as a memory in my flesh,
as I descend
back down to do my work.
I let the simplest pleasure charm my gut.
I anthropomorphize passions in nature
and try to remember to let belief evaporate.

Destroyer

HOW AWKWARDLY
one must sacrifice so many
probable realities
for the sake of each moment.
So many deaths precede
due to the singular goal of man.
I have been a murderer.
I have killed my young mother
and so many lovers.
I watched their form collapse
under a single word
or limp beneath a lengthy sentence
attempting to excuse the willingness
to turn away from a future so promising,
so absolutely perfect.
Perfect as the unknown
blurry uncharted paths
I fear to wander through.
I will not go unless I can not see where it leads
and so the dense assumptions must die.
Die by my hand. Die by my pen.
Much has been sacrificed
for the sake of my higher self.
One thousand silent friends.
One thousand lustless beds
buried in the imagination
of what could have been.

Good morning

EVERYTHING IS NEW
The world is an endless question.
that I receive *minuet* answers.
I hold them in my mind for milliseconds.
I hold them like infants.
I let their babble run though my mouth
into a stream of consciousness
that flows into another
and becomes larger.
The small talk loses itself in vastness.
I simultaneously fear the power
as I tread in awe and reverence.
I forget my questions.
I forget the answers.
I am
swimming inside of the great gut of nature.
My form, my muscles are tired after some time so I return to shore.
For warm rest in the sand and familiars who prefer to dwell in land.
Until the ocean calls to me again.
I am safe.
I am always presented with exactly what I need.

I don't know any of these things

HOW ARE YOU DOING
with those wounds.
How have you come
to the acceptance of your greatness.
How has your warrior
taken your innocent orphan
into their arms and assured
them that they will be safe.
Has your seeker become
starved enough.
Has he gone to your children
and said that you are now
going to fall off of the sphere
of everything that you have known
in search of a different form of sustenance.
Did you kiss your mothers goodbye.
Did you pull the cord
and tell them you would return
with new eyes.
Did you burn your portraits
and did you pack a sketchbook
to scratch every angle of new longing.
Did you decide to be alone
instead of lonely.
Did you decide to be full.
Did you write your government.
Did you dream your fathers over coffee
and tell them that you are going
going to find more evolved men
to emulate.
How are you doing

with your stories of heartache.
Do you still ruminate and repeat them
over and over,
again and again.
Do you still believe that you are
somehow damaged.
Do you still seek solace and healing in the wombs
of young women.
Have you decided to be reborn
or do you keep hiding your head inside of them
playing ghost under their sheets.
Are you afraid of the shadows
you hid behind the moon.

I don't know any of these things.
I just hope you have chosen to become
a hero again.

Unspoken

THERE IS A PERFECT.
There is an expectation.
There are illusions.
I could define them
in some metaphor,
in some stanzas.
I could take on articulating them.
I am coaxed into realms without language.
going with things my gut just knows.
Intuitions are impeded by the slowness of my pen.
Bliss is lost in the audible sounding of vowels.
Interpretation swindles a reader's freedom.
This poem is already too long.

Paint thighs

SOMETHING OF NO SENSE.
Something crude.
Something illegible
Goddamn, I wish.
I wish I never thought I needed to.

Park sitting

I LONG FOR THE DAYS
when my pen ran across clean white pages
to produce honest romance.
Now it is a challenge to express pure love.
I argue amongst my selves
with doubt and uncertainty.
Once love ran through my hands
and back out of my mouth
so that my words were small glowing songs
illuminating the skin, face, and eyes of the night.
Now I conjure details that create shadowy images.
One must bring their own candle to be serenaded
only to be filled with questions and released again.
I long for the days when truths were simple,
when it would not sore or sour my throat to speak them.

Random mind vomit

I BORROWED THEIR IDEAS, AND CHOICE OF CIGARETTES
I kept them with me that way
after we got out of our one-night bed.
I have never been so free,
so without a dear close friend to share
countless nights.
There's a pop punk band to bounce to
downtown every other night.
I try to shake my half moon sacral wide.
It caves in after meeting so many
tired drunken eyes.
I send my old love letters
over astral planes,
then I wake to find them returned
after bouncing off his numb tired heart.
I find unconditional love in morning cigarettes.
I am perceived only as a physical thing.
I cannot wait for my energy to go boundless
under the man-made apocalypse of consumption.

So many beautiful truths.
So many perforated portals
I hardly speak but once every three times I'm spoken to.
I grow wary of vibrant syllables.

Silliness

WHAT A STRANGE THING
I keep the light on for.
A silent knowing.
This forever loving.
Heart so open
it stings in pieces
to re-mend
as a muscle
that re-strings itself
and tunes
to make harmony in a grander octave.
So much higher than ever
heard sung.
I empty and open
and become a mound
that slowly piles into a mountain.
Earth, but also water.
A lake that learns to become a sea.
Have I grown wide enough now.
Aren't I churning?
Frail anxieties
inhabit my poetry.
I float out in a torrent
with waterproof pen
awaiting to be consumed
by my self-created sea.
Great green monster
with your many unpredictable limbs.
I want to be struck by one accidental swing,
and swallowed whole.
I want to experience circulation again,

free from my paralyzed inertia.
Circling the moon
and making believe
it is a sun.

Ssssshhhhh

I TELL THE WATERS TO BE STILL.
I drown in creation.
Turn off the moon and the stars.
Startle me with my own darkness.
Earth has become too soft beneath my feet
and my mind is fertile
with glowing epiphanies
that hold no symbol or sound
but slide down through my core
and fill my body with warmth.
My bedroom light is dim upon the late summer night.
I am unaware of the four walls that bind me.
My front door is wide open
and the waves are sliding in and soaking the carpet.
The sofa rocks gently above the floor.
Tell me something you are sure of.
Speak to me about science, and the *Declaration*.
I have remembered what I am.
Full of glory.
I am bursting seamlessly.
I own the depth and space that surrounds me.
Why don't you psychoanalyze me.
Tell me I am dancing in illusion.
Set a text book on my lap so that I do not float
through the ceiling.
Let the night be over.
I wish it had never come.
Let the sun blaze upon every surface
so that I am confused by how many things there are.
So that I can not recall the simplicity of the essence in
things.

I cannot share the night.
It is too vast to fathom.
You may be tempted to siphon
the amber sap from my trees
and lap milk from the stars.
A taste too sweet,
you will be forever home.
You would lay down and pulse with inescapable bliss.
There is no reason in ecstasy.
Flip on a harsh fluorescent light,
turn on the television,
and bother yourself with all of humanity.

The brick wall

HERE'S TO YOU,
never spending a moment alone.
You seek distraction in bars
where you drink yourself
into a numbness.
Incapable of feeling
the overstimulation
of so much pounding
small talk.

Here's to you,
never finding time to feel
the silence and the sacredness
of your limbs
and the ghost of your breath.

You,
never took the time
to listen to yourself
or find out what you think.

You,
deaf and blind
to the pattern,
the agenda,
all of your lessons.
Here's to you,
I tried to hear your heart
but I only got static and dead air.
I undressed you once,
but I could not find your soul.

The last one

I TOLD MY BEST MALE FRIEND WE WOULD
meet up once we were eighty
and share a life together.
That way we could taste everyone and everything
without restraint.

I said,
maybe you don't believe in the one
but I'm going to be the last one.
We're going to love each other and share a bed one
morning
and the next we'll be dead.
That's the closest to holy union
either of us is going to get.

The shadow sage

LET ME STAY IN MY MIND
where so many pristine portraits
are created vivid
one conscious stroke at a time.
Do not drag your fingers over the oily impressions.
You are not permitted into this exhibit
because you are so tempted.

Let me be in pure infatuation
where all of my desires, all of my destinations
are whole and exactly as they seem.

This is *anima, animus.*
This is my idyllic garden,
forever quenched,
forever blooming.

Your eyes would shift the scene.
Your thoughts would touch the petals
of my rose bushes
and they would shudder in introduction.
They would shrivel if you were not gentle,
if you threatened to prune them too soon.
Pluck one, and you have tipped
their effortless equilibrium.

Let me have my dreams exactly as they seem,
Let me make love with my perfect masculine,
here, in the garden:
in my womb, in my heart, in limbic,
hovering above the crown of my head.

Your presence would cause interference.
Leave me, in peace,
in a reality
you could not comprehend
without so many questions.

Mind dissects.
Vocabulary isolates whole things
in loose translations.
It is painful, to know
that once you are interpreted
you have been fragmented.

Leave me being.
All is well here
in sanctuary.
Mind your own.
Tend and till.
Know how sacred
peace of mind is.
Know how the shadow
and bloom
become one.

Then, then maybe you would
thank the ground
and ask forgiveness
before treading on it.
Maybe then, you would thank my skin
before touching it.
Maybe then, gratitude and genuine care
would not be foreign to you.

This is my poem for today

EVEN THOUGH I DON'T WRITE POEMS
this is my stream of words for the day.
Written in linear fashion.
Maybe I could write a book
and get famous.
I'm uncertain.
I can hardly get my point across
this way
and other ways.
Here is my poem for the day.
I hope you like it.

Waiting for a plane

I HAVE RETURNED
from displacement
to find myself
happily disconnected
from these blank pages.

They are no longer a reflection
of my bland expression.

My thoughts
are vibrant
and fluid.
Churning and existing
to quench my boredom.

Satisfying me
whether or not
they take form
through my pen.

I have found myself
in adventure again.

Zen is a three-letter word

HOW WE SPOKE.
How another fear was conditioned into me.
In hindsight I see
everything
in bias,
in half truth
and a sea.

Scripts scribbled on the shores,
devoured by the strengths
of constant ebb.
Creating the faint flashbulb,
uncertainty,
incomplete.
I take the ghostly impressions
with me.
Heavy in the back
of my mind.
Called out to negotiate,
each coming stance,
each predetermined movement.

I may as well be tethered
at the wrists and ankles.
Directed by a looming crowd of
shadowy faces, calloused hands
and omniscient projection.
I cling desperately to a belief
in non-belief.
I rewrite agreements again
and again

to make myself clean.
History still has not left me.
The past tugs at the back of my knees
and my ideals drift carelessly
in a breeze
coming in from the future.
I would not mislead you
by stating
that I am here now.
I would not lie
and tell you that I am grounded.
I could not say
that I was not
tainted at birth.
Form is in my bones.
Samsara devoured me
in the fluorescent flames
of a sterile east coast hospital ward.
and I am only human.
I feel things.

The pendulum rocks
inside my chest
and cradles me to sleep.
The constant movement
keeps me up most nights
'til my eyes itch
from being so long
in silence.
I take one glance
at the truth
that I seek
and hide it in a dream
as I go to work

in my unconscious.
I am •
the soft flesh
that embodies history
if not,
the future would be
exactly as it seemed
the moment my eyes fluttered
in waking dream.

Her love

LOVE GROWS HER
tends her,
seeds her
nurtures her.

Seasons turn and she stretches,
and sleeps soft in cold earth.

Her heart
remains delicate.
Wet with all inspiration or tears,
electric with passion
and righteous with god.

Her love is beauty alone.

02232012

THE WANDERER IS FINALLY STILL.
His face weathered into a stony, stern expression.
His body tired and willing to be swaddled
in a warm cocoon where rest regenerates.
His forehead creased like a washboard
where he will scrub the recollections clean from his garments.
Wringing out each mark left by sudden disturbance;
an unsteady hand with a glass of whiskey
that soils his coat,
dark earth left on his hind pockets
from sitting outside in a courtyard at sunrise
waiting for the cafe to open.
It is time to be still and silent,
as he recalls each frenzied dream
that led his journey.
Dreams that intertwine with reality.
Inner talk muffled against the echoes of true occurrences.
He settles into a town he is fond of
and makes a home with kind hearts,
who feed him and wonder
where his mind goes in his silence.
They once saw him teaching their boy
how to speak to autumn leaves
and know the decomposition they lend.
He was a curious middle-aged man
who was waiting to be orphaned again.
Orphaned, by the few lovers he managed to seduce
with his last wind of delicious adventurousness.
Lovers like ripe fruit

which he stored for the winter, and grew thin
as the vividness of their memories depleted.
When every memory of their lingering comforts
have been sucked frail.
When the sheets have lost the scent
of their perfume.
When the child goes out to play with the dogs.
When the neighbors grow tired of chipping away
at his many walls.
He will go see again,
which truths can be obtained
from the exits of the evening train.

03252012i

PROMISE THAT YOU WILL HELP ME SABOTAGE THIS.
Not one more step,
until we both agree
that this will end
abrupt and half-hearted.
We are willing to plunge into the vulnerable depths
that supply our longing with fodder for art.
Our passions blaze across this continent
leaving our homelands barren,
clean and new.
Left with tales of old land.
Mourning long enough
to write our tragic ballads.
Mourning until we are bored of grieving.

03252012ii

IT'S NEVER TRUE.
It's never romance,
or the comfort
of our religious upbringings.
The blissful arrogance
of childhood dreams,
handed to us
in the vintage handkerchiefs
of our grandmothers.

Wear your cross as a disguise.
Undress yourself.
Give your body to me as sacrifice.
Pull your crucifix to your bare chest.
Make love to me
as if you will be crucified
come sunrise.
Any man with eight beers in him
is the second coming.
and I will participate in your blasphemy,
as long as you feed my hunger
for loss and longing.

Be an absent god
and I will moan.
As long as you promise
to leave me.

As long as you promise
to leave me.

04012012

TERRIFIED OF ROMANCE
opting for cognitive debate
the monotonous exchange of sterile ideas
calculating how primal of a moan
will be allowed to slip
from
the
lips,
as if
triturating how much soul
can be uncovered.
Spirits sit up in the tree
above my bedroom window
smirking at how empty
the lovers moved within us.
They allow us to pretend.
How long can we stand
giving only half truth
and fearful persona
before we grow bored.
How long will we agree
to undressing in dry desolation.
Our urgency kept hidden
and coaxed with scolding hisses
back into the shadows
of folded organs.
How long until we reach
for the comfort
of aching poetry
scrawled to save the lives
of drowning muses.

How long until we allow the inspiration
they disowned to lead less vulnerable lives
animate our senses.
How long until we allow the lovers to lend
their breath to the muses once more
to create
the eternal present.

04052012

THE WHITE WALLS REFLECTED LIGHT DIFFERENTLY
in the ocean motel bathroom.
Blank canvas that did not weaken her soul:
though her timid heart exhausted
and dehydrated from turning her memoirs
over in her desert grave.

The man who was no longer her lover
sprawled out long and thin
on the hideous acrylic queen comforter:
left foot limp from hanging on the gas for eight hours.

It was a long drive,
for a short trip to
retrieve her spirit.

Which she may have
left in a caked glass pipe
that shattered on the curb
in front of her adopted brother's crash pad.
She may have left it in a deep hole
in the sand beneath a thick layer of seaweed
and a cloud of buzzing flies.
Or pushed it back
into the throat of a one night stand
with her tongue.
Perhaps he sang it loose at the Portugalia
and it was unknowingly kicked off stage
and down the steps onto the salty sweat strip
in Ocean Beach.

In the cabinet-sized bathroom
where she hid to think too loudly,
the intoxicating scent of the ocean filled her nostrils
through the cloudy cracked window
and let her mind float in a nine a.m. fog.

Wouldn't it be fun
to make love in the motel room?
She asks.

No,
I'm tired.

She stretches out on the bed beside him
and puts her head on his chest
but his body feels stiff
and all of the fabrics are scratching her skin.
She fingers the buttons on his collared shirt,
and wonders if he causes
her hunger and discomfort.

His scent does not make her
drunk enough to sing
any longer.
It fills her gut
with sour milk
and turns her stomach
before their leaky boat
leaves shore.

She hates to touch him,
and she hates that her body
belongs to him.
She knows

that no matter where she goes
this unnameable unhappiness will persist.

4. *Mercury in Aries*

05042012

MY LOVER SCARES MY GHOSTS AWAY,
wraps my haunted body up in his arms
and they scatter like smoke into the night.
Once he has gone
I ask them to return.
They hang their cobwebs up in my ribcage.
They track their tar along my lungs
until I cough up ink blots
that I pretend to see my old lovers' faces in.
I curl up warm in familiar heartache.
I write of longing with shaky hands.
Calling them back to feel melancholy again.
To hear my name whispered in the braille of his fingerprints
on the steel strings of jazz records.

05072012

LET ME BORROW AN EVENING.
Come have a beer.
I'll sit across from you at the bar
and mirror your posture,
borrow your gestures
and stories.

Let me see the way you
hold your cigarette.
Let me imagine the way you
hold your pen.
Though I may never glimpse
your evening rendezvous
with a gallon of wine
and the magic of imagination.

You may never spy on my
watery dance through
the dimly lit apartment
on the balls of my feet
as the old records spin.
Nina and Mitchell.
Blue and violet
in my hips.

Let me walk through
the lectures that echo
in the great halls of your mind.
I will go as a stowaway
and listen intently
in the back corner

to the stories told by our peers,
young men and women
keeping the print alive.

Let me be a voyeur,
long enough to wear your pants
and write with your hands.
I am a good reporter.
I will slip your persona on
like a silk dress
and wear it so that
I can feel into your shadowy secrets.

One more drink,
a book list,
and we can both be
on our way.

05092012

GIVE ME YOUR WOUNDS.
I will dress them.
Give me your sorrows,
I will drain them.
Hang them out to dry
and sew a clean pair of garments
to mine for diamonds in coal with.
I will decipher your language,
giving it back in poetry.
Undress, and I will move
all of the muscles in your form.
I will unwind every tense thing you've clung to.
Give me what has aged in you,
I will iron it out.
I won't trust you with mine.

Give me your heart,
I will cradle it in my palms.
I will swallow it without teeth.
I will run a razor delicately along your lungs
to remove the tar.
I will dust the cobwebs from your ribcage.
I will reset the sun so that it is shone
into the center of your crown.
Do not ask to see inside my chest
it is open long enough to indulge in your healing
but snaps like a mouse trap upon fingers
that reach in.
I won't trust you with mine.

05162012

WOKE THIS MORNING TO A STORM RAGING
in the right hemisphere of my mind.
Feeling my lover drown himself in its ocean,
I shed a tear that landed on the top of my foot.
A wave came to pull it in,
blessing his cheek.
He sank below layers of knowing.
Gorgeous Ophelia,
lost again,
hidden in depths of plagiarized literature.
Forsaken.
Anger rose in my stomach
and brought a flood of hot tears.
I pulled my muscles in tight
readying myself for the day's work.
There is no time to mourn the dead.

05162012ii

KISS ME WITH YOUR SERPENT TONGUE
without jaw or venom.
Suckle at my breast
without tasting milk.
Climb the linear notches of my spine
with your catskill claws
without drawing blood.
Quench the thirst of my roots
showing through barren soil
with water you walk six miles
from the canal
without bringing a sip to your lips.
Devour me, murderously
with your eyes
but do not let me catch your concentration
with a swift glance.
Love me, eternally
without ever waking in my bed.
Allow me to bear your fantasies
in a pregnant star
we watch die
at the center of a distant desert.
Keep me as a folktale dream
you've folded deep into places
where there are only symbols.
Keep me as a faint melody
that reflects at the back of your globe-like eyes.
Lick ocean rain from your skin
and taste the salt as tears
that you shed once you lost my love
by speaking my name.

05302012i

I PUT MY WRITER AWAY MONTHS AGO
to keep myself from telling truths.
To keep myself from rage and disappointment.
The black and white of written language
are the frames of lines and angles that hold up whole possible worlds
where I cake oil pastels on the interior
and create scaffolding for exhibition.
I put my writer away
so that I wouldn't have to know my own pain.
I stuffed her in an old suitcase
and decided I would take her back out once I had changed.
Once she was hidden
there was no one to tell me whether I was happy.
There was no one to show me my restlessness.
Some nights I would hear her pounding
from the back of my closet
objecting to the man in my bed.
Screaming, shouting,
shouting muffled warnings.
All my ears were saturated in wine
and I slept her off
until her voice went hoarse.
She began to resent me.
I am alone again.
I take her out to ask how it was
all those months in forced muteness.
She just looks at me with disgusted silence.
There are no reports for the records.
Nothing to show for a life half-done.

And my writer,
she's abandoned me.

06042012

I GET LONELY WHEN I'M ALONE
and try to see the trees breathe
but there's a brick in my diaphragm
and an iron casing around my pituitary.
I want to see their leaves glow again.
I want to talk to spiders
and feel my eight legs inching along.
I want to smell Gaia's warm milk
in the dirt between my toes.
I want to gaze at hummingbirds suspended in time
and watch the light that glows in their chest.
Where has my magic gone?
I would like to ask the flowers how their diets are.
My romance goes flat.
Longing to contemplate fields
and dance among forms.
Humming to the tune of spines.
I'd like to feel the pulse of consciousness again
but I have gone numb in my sadness.
I do not move inside the
rhythm of what's living.

06162012ii

IN THE MOUTHS OF WOLVES
digested back into
Gaia's soft womb.
and unearthed again
as a delicate clay vase
with braille Latin etchings.
I brush my fingertips against it
and it lets out
a sticky low sound
that makes my phantom limb howl
as if it were torn again.
Symphonies I did not know
I could write any longer.
Strangers wander into my forest
during spring
expecting fields and gardens
after a distant winter.
They trample mammals' dens
and devour sparrows' eggs.
Wildflowers are plucked,
stamen's powder coated their tongues.
Honeysuckles are licked clean.
They become a dense
unrecognizable collection
of leaves.
My kingdom in shambles.
My creatures all question my reign.
They've left a bit of pulp for paper,
and sap for tea.
They've juiced all of the black berries for ink.
Besides, I could not stomach

the documentation of the pillage of this place.
The silent text books
bare secrets of what flourished
and what was taken.

06232012iii

YOUR VOICE DIED IN LOUISIANA
You swallowed the swamp,
used the ink for your articles.
You couldn't sing.
You taught your hand
how to glide along the frets
of a semi-hollow body.
You didn't know enough covers to play a gig.
You wrote of the musicians in New Orleans,
they never thanked you.
Your column read by a faithful five.
You soaked the jazz into your humid pores
and perspired in the stiff white sheets
of the women who could still smell your pheromones
through the stench of piss and liquor
that saturated red creole brick streets.
When the flood came
you stopped taking your father's calls.
Swore you would stay to save the lost souls
and pale for their notes in the flooded alleys.
But your father, he got through to make you return.
While held up in his sterile suburban home
you mimicked the sounds you loved.
You rewrite their notes and
you tinker with their influence.
You throw on their twang and form the chords.
Desert rats devour your blues and jazz.
They furrow with your folk
and their eyes sweat with
your memories of humid culture.

07072012

I WANTED TO JUMP THROUGH THE WINDOW
of the propeller room,
chop myself into little pieces
through the blades of the fan,
and land on the cold street
of an old mountain town.
It was too cold to make it through the window
so I stayed under the covers
with my head on a new bare chest.
The heat of mammalian skin, polar
to the elevated autumn chill.
I wake from a daze of comfort internally screaming,
The symbols are dead!
The symbols are dead!

I want to die.
I want to hang myself from the roof
of the barn,
where *anahata* is lit up aflame
in Walmart clearance holiday lights.
Meaning has been strangled,
gasping for breath
like the haggard cough of a moonshiner
and his fellow pothead.

An army of illiterates
have been employed to create the myths
of our generation.

—

"my flesh is heretic,

my body is a witch,
I am burning it".

07092012ii

I STUCK A TOE INTO THE COLORADO RIVER
And heard my brothers song in tongues
that climbed up my leg and spine
like a great snake.
He did not sing me a sermon
or twist tales of romantic sins,
I felt his soul, I knew his feeling.
Once he was mysterious.
Initiated my capacity to harm myself.
A capacity to negotiate healing.
My catalyst.
Our relation has shifted a dozen times over this decade
like the river his soul flows to greet me in.
I know his song well,
I know his blues,
even when it comes in new tones.
I recognize the sound of his fingerprints
against the coil of steel strings.

07092012iii

MI CARINA, MI DIOSA, LA MAR
I feel my spirit being pried away from you
as we speed through the desert in this car.
It was just hours ago that I danced upon your lips,
mi carina.
Your breath is the pulse of my heart
and the perspiration of my light, *mi diosa.*
I have come here to worship.
I have come to wrap myself in your womb.
To feel the strength of my mother
and be reborn, *la mar.*
Me descanso en las palmas en la final.

07112012

A PACK OF CIGARETTES
neat and modern.
Sleek, thick paper,
rows of white.
Memories of waking
to know what the day was for.
On this one
we are not sure.
We see all of our habits,
addictions and idiosyncrasies,
clearly.

A series of objects to attach the self to:
a pen, a piece of paper, friction.
A gas stove, ground beans, boiling water,
a familiar earthy aroma.
A shelf of books
the mind is too hazy to comprehend.
We worry about our lovers
again, again.
A new record, a bit of tobacco.

Life is done like this.
This is the way we wake in the morning.
Though we do not know
what the day is for.
Not anymore.

07142012

ANDREW,
my ankles are bare.
Watch how they
turn like the ocean.
My heels are calloused.
ignore them, I might be numb.

I did not know how hot I could get
until I woke one morning
with the white sheet wrapped around our legs.
I had a fever in the springtime.
You tried to put a cold wet cloth over my forehead,
to soothe the sickness.
I say no.
You send me home with my guitar case.

Rusty plays slide and Wilco,
he plays the songs
that put sweetness on my tongue.
He takes me to the breakers,
teaches me how to paddle out.

And Andrew, why do you push me away,
Quoting *Independence Day*.
Asking me to abandon my muse.

Just allow me to listen to you think.
Give me a riff, an afternoon witnessing
the curiosity that pours out of you.

Andrew.

07142012i

I'VE DRUNK TOO MUCH
tongued the pills
I swore I would not touch.
I touched them.
I touched you.
I touched you
when your eyes fluttered
in your mountain kitchen.
The tile wet by the sink
you tracked small gray prints
from the puddle
on the way back to your room.
I couldn't bear to follow you there.
Not into the bed,
where a stack of scrawled journals
and books lay in the passenger side.
Not the down comforter!
Nor the shadows whispering secrets
and invitations
from the orange bulb of a single lamp.
It may be a sin.
An eradication of boundaries,
set to keep us silent, contently apart.
My mouth is dry,
I keep my lips from wrapping around destructive things.
No limbic assimilation of your sweat!

07232012

DRIFTING THROUGH FOLK IMAGERY
I look up past my sail,
wipe the fog from my glasses
put all my trinkets and heirlooms
back away in their cabinets
in no particular order.

I see a young man whose
eyes are glazed and transfixed
on our entertainment.
I admire his daydream
and scan the room,

observing that
every being in the building
is the center of their collapsed universe.
Massive intersections
of invisible cord,
tangled and feeding,
Pumping –
Nourishing –
In tune –

I place a scrawled message into a syringe
and inject it into a single heart string.
I send it coursing into the collective bosom.
I love you ...
I love you ...
I love you ...

07252012

HE COULD NOT HAVE KNOWN ME.
I had not known myself.
Mediocre poetry.
All the time spent in silence
and forever camping on the cool tile
of our studio bathroom
to escape him.

Surely a two-year collection of these
creates a single great work.
I am not sure.
Our journal left
on the bottom shelf of an ancient closet
may be discovered by new tenants.
They may attempt to decipher
our transcriptions and notations.

My works are saturated with him.
My pen knotted to my fingers
with his long dark hair.
I want to play a new tune.
I try to ignore his imagery
but it swells up inside of me
and forces his influence
through my fingerprints.
I try to clean the sheets
but my dreams cause me to sweat him out of me.

The men I've loved guide me as muses
in child's romantic fantasia.

There is no more room
in the major arcana.

07292012

THE PORCH WAS WELL LIT.
Fluorescent.
An excavation illuminated
around me.
I slid the key into the knob
and found the lock was free.
Silently padding the few feet to my bedroom,
I watched my mother's sleeping breath
on my living-room floor,
gently sealing the door behind myself.
I removed each piece of clothing,
wrapped my stones around their pillar
to rest and be cleansed.
My cheek grazed the pillow,
sleep flooded my body.
Still, something was absent.
I was anxious, searching
For the piece that would let me be still.
Wrapping my arm around the pillow
I discover that it was him.
The cotton was reestablished
as the faint memory of his chest,
while I attempted to reconstruct
the scent of his skin.
I created a shoddy recall
of dreaming soundly
in his arms and drifted off.
Content to deceive my own longing.

08042012ii

THE COUPLE WAS AT A FRIEND'S HOME
drinking vodka and playing Scrabble.
She laid on the living room rug
On her back as *Dark Side* spun
on the turn table.
Her boyfriend exclaimed
that the female vocal solo
at the end of the great gig was
"excessive".
She rolled her eyes behind her closed lids
and wondered how she could help him see
that the passions and their expression
were indispensable.

She laid back on the carpet
allowing the woman's voice
to run up her spine
and down her neck
and arms.
She felt her final wail
reverberate in her hips.

08242012

SHE'S TOO PRETTY FOR YOU.
Maybe you love her well.
Maybe not.
Your smooth boyish skin
glows through a cloud of cigarette smoke.
How many wrinkles does a man require
to know how to love a woman.
He must be submerged in her psyche
and nearly drowned to reincarnate.
He should leave the bathtub carved into deep deep
grooves.
He should be sailed to the center of the Atlantic
and left to be retrieved by the thousandth passing ship
that finally takes pity on him.

08282012

NO PARTNERS FOR CRIME.
No crime
in a place where
apathy is valued above passion.

Passion is crime
and apathy,
Zen.

Zen
a form of violence
aborting the coming
revolution's germination.

My passions blaze
confined within the belly of a saxophone
nearly branding my player's lips
flames doused by the omnipotent intellect.

Omnipotence:
claims there was no war,
no rally, no riot;
that tore the mailbox holding ballots
from neighborhood lawns.
I saw fascists:
burning open mic sign-ups.
I found overdue gas bills in a flash flood puddle.
I found my words gathered in cysts
under my collarbone.

There is only a riot

when you predict,
the calm claim
there will be no predictions of riots.

No partners for crime.
No crime in a place where
apathy is valued over passion.

No art in a place where apathy
condemns passion.

The local news is scripted.
They edited the war on the hedonistic,
swore the artists drank themselves to death.

According to the elite:
the bohemians chose their own exit.

08292012

MY EYELIDS ARE TALKING AGAIN,
they whisper, eye love yous.
My pupils glance off
making up futures.

My brain aches
in seeking memories
encrypted in our DNA.
Binary Latin
that reports archaic infantile
cave-drawling babble.

Please, don't be afraid of me.
Please, don't name me entropy.
Please, don't say I inhibit your dreams.
I'll only inhabit one or two a night.

I don't understand how I know your soul so soon.
I don't understand how I've loved you already,
before.

08312012

I WAKE UP IN THE MORNING
the whole world hurts.

It's the middle of the night,
the whole world hurts.

The sun's blazing
over two p.m. pavement,
the whole world hurts.

The last thing I need,
is my own personal pain.

09262012

THEY SAID
say nothing if I'd nothing nice to say
I have beautiful things to say
but I cannot say them.
The truth comes in pairs
in this place there is a twoness to experience.
All the separate things
illuminated by the sun
so far far away.
All the separate things.
I breathe them in.
Particle invisibles
nestle themselves
in my lungs
speckled by tar.
I want to speak.
My throat is too full.
There are too many things
to speak for.
I can speak for myself ... myself,
what is that?
I married my bed.
I married the city.
I dreamed myself one
with the fog of streetlights.
I tried to love it all.
I embraced the one.
My arms got sore.
Its whiskey breath choked me.
Get me to the nearest open space
let me view the stars and moon

in two dimensions.
When I am ready,
let me be frightened to know
that they are only partially
illuminated.
And let me call their darkness
faulty.
Let me hate the darkness within me.
Let me go mad in isolation.
Let me tear myself into pieces.
Let me tear myself into pieces
with the belief in pieces
with the belief,
in separate things.
And when I miss being whole
perhaps I will look at the stars
and the moon
and say,
"How vaguely beautiful!"
And when I miss the city
let me go back and see its beauty.
Perhaps, then
I will know how
to love all things.

11112012:1226pm

I AM IN LOVE WITH THE SPILLING OF PASSIONS
with the release of them.
I am in love with what something becomes
after it is gone.
I am in love with memories given
as gifts wrapped in art.
I am in love with that
and the timelessness
that threads it.
The threads to hang the self with.
The threads to cut my dry little fingers on.

I am in love with gone.

Just as my lover is gone.
Gone in a syringe.
Gone in a dimension where he dances with philosophy.
Gone with his true love on eternal vacation.

When he returns he wagers me for
the high price of reality.

The price of trite.
The price of rebellion.
The price of young.
The price of seeking.
The price of woman.

My lover could take or leave me.
He leaves me mostly.
And when he takes me,

he takes me with fear.
He takes me with stiff calloused hands
and sore arms.

He takes me
with a dozen medicines
coursing through him
so that he can say it was not him.

When my lover loves
he gives his love to another woman.
He writes his poetry to her.
When he sees beauty he gives it to her.
He gives Beauty her name.
He names her love and joy,
pleasure and bliss.

He looks at me with a straight face
as I remove my clothing.
I dance, I sing,
expose my soul;
and it is not enough.
I could not be named Love by him.

I am nothing here.
Nothing hears me here.
Nothing knows me here.

I could shine like anything.
I could shine like the brightest diamond.
I could be the brightest diamond
and he would not know it.

If I stay I will be dull.

I would make a dull life.
Packed away in his boxes
collecting dust.

I would die condoning his heroins,
the needle and the faint memory
of a woman seen through its afterglow.

I could tongue the foggy window pane.
I would rather run my hard breasts
against the freezing surface
of the full length mirror

than press my bare heart
against the chest of a man
who thinks me some sort of dead thing.
Some kind of thing that cannot be known.

A thing that can be named
and put away.
A thing that can be ignored.

I am in love with gone.

11172012:pm

TINY WOUNDED BABBLE TALES
loop delicately around the base of sleeping cobras.
A bit of weight to keep the body here.
Body full of
mind, heart, soul
and a child's confusion.

Confusion of the wise
leaning upon the infant.
The pressure makes
dense trinkets to be disclosed.

Each time they are transcribed
with the trembling fingers
of wary readiness
a layer of cocoon
becomes moth dust
as it is chipped away
with the angel-thin fingernails of embryo.

Within an eternal metaphor two float
in some womb
defined with dream.

The warm liquid
coaxes suffering to the lips
that sing sweet ballads
to each other's children.

May-uh, may-uh.
Tah-tuh-tah.

Twoness
wondering at vibrant mirrors,
secretly hiding disbelief
that any scar could reside
in the spirit of presence.

Two with compassion
bless one another
in still silence
that holds the beauty of all
with hollow strength.

In awe with itself,
in awe at how beauty
and love can be known
by two people,
gently realizing a subtle unwinding,
an unfolding of
a loose sensation of divinity.

11222012:0220am

IT MAY BE A SURE THING
that there is an essence in form.
That there is a pillar of light
that suspends the bodies,
trees, and dimensions floating,
strung like beads.
Mother of pearl, jade,
a stone one may need to listen with.

Medicine strings
one could wear round their neck
to lay upon the heart.
A reminder of how the earth knows all about
a human, animal, or person thing.

An inanimate could hold the wake
of tempered grief.
One could feel sadness or joy in grass,
in birds, in babies.

This sort of fullness
is wholly,
to be brimming
with resonance.

The seas in these places
rock a captain to sickness.

And still its vibrant color,
a collage, a turning inside-out.
An open view of what is.

The essence in things
can string a spine right back up from that.
Its grace a light hand from a cloud
could pull the hair from wet cheeks
and it could rest itself silently on cold skin.

Koan

I LOVE YOU TOO MUCH
and I have never touched you.
but I have known your soul.
Your soul has known me.

I have birthed too many poems
with your suns inside of them.

I let go partially,
I feel sparks kick back a bit
to silence and request
a pretty smile for the celibate king.

I hold your poems in thought.
They are like many suns.

I grin at them,
squinting.
All of your suns
too hot inside of me.

Commencing

THE SHAMAN ATTUNED US
with his ceremony speech.

We each stepped forward
to taste what he called,
Grandmother.

A galactic womb!

We drunk her muddy water.
One by one, many.
Turning, round and round we went!
I imagined the taste was licorice.

I sat with my spine deep in the earth.
With closed eyes I felt a mother's presence.

Churning, churning.
Making little stars in me,
projecting constellations
on the backs of my eyelids.

From deep in her soft bosom
I heard a howling coming.
Howling from the dark
crevices of mountains.
Moaning deep and wild.
Licking sharp teeth
with pupils wide
to devour my stars!

I knew there were wolves dancing,
off in the distance.
I made a play with them.
Fed them my right hand.
Allowed them to lap at my joy.

And galaxies thanked me
as the wolves did.
And the galaxies said,
you have done your deed.
Now sleep,
sleep,
and mothers will hold you tenderly.

Excerpt from tonight's rant

COME HERE HONEY,
let me put you in my sex box.
Which manufactured flavors do you subscribe to?
Can I purchase your chapstick at the corner store
and snack on it while I'm stalking your OkCupid profile?
There's a world full of people,
they're falling off the flatland like a waterfall.
I've had brunch with a new woman every day this week
and still, I'm lonely.
There are no American poets.
There is no food of sustenance
in this suburban sprawl of chain restaurants.

*F*lg*r*

I LEFT LITTLE **** BLOSSOMS
of **** on *** *** white ******.

I **** one of my short ***** *****
On his ****** wall
Beside the two long ****** strands left by *** old ****.

Next time I am *******
*** **** from my *****,
I will recheck the tally.

Calling beauty a "cunt"

SOMEONE WALKS INTO THE ROOM AND TELLS YOU TO
stop crying so loud.
It's six a.m., you'll wake the neighbors.
You're a child now,
what do you WANT?

You think on it,
what DO you want?
And you cry more,
because
no one has it
no one has what you REALLY want.

Someone tells you everyday to
shut the fuck up.
It's selfish to speak.
It's selfish to feel your own feelings.
You're selfish.
You're taking up space.

So STOP.
FUCKING.
CRYING.

Quit being a pussy.

It isn't so bad.
You're not from here.

You're a goddamn angel.
An alien.

You're a spirit.
You're not your ego.
You're not your feelings.
You're certainly not that fucking dress.

So stop
acting
like a
cunt.

Stop feeling.

Quit being a woman.

STOP
FUCKING
CRYING.

Stop behaving
like a
god
damned
human.

For Rumi and Han Shan

MY MASTERS WENT UP ON THE MOUNTAIN
and learned to love their longing
so that they felt no pain of human passions
in the many forms they took.

They were ancient thin scavengers
who longed to fill the gaping hole of want and desire.
My masters lived in cold shacks
and made love to the koan of their teachers.
They chased god
and left the present with their pens
to create works
that would mislead me to believe
that they found such romance in physical things
and died beside their lovers.

Old male pacifists,
who toiled with nothing
but their own inner landscapes.
Who crafted words from dreams
and a deep-seated escapism.

Galaxy spine

THE WAY TO GOD IS IN THE SPINE.
All communion with one begins in meditation.
It comes from the soul realizing itself,
and the soul allowing itself to bypass the trappings of
self.

Any conflict with the self and soul creates
an obstruction in the perception of god.

God without assumptions.
God that is not hungry.
God without a face or agenda.

That is the god I find myself held by in moments
of clarity.

A god that does not hold.
A god that does not let go.

Once I return,
I know that all is illusive.
even I am illusive.
Once I return I am separate.
I begin to feel unique.
This is the first boundary I cross
to leave enlightenment behind.

Differences make grief.
Differences make friction.
They make conversation.
They make longing.

They make struggle.

In wholly union,
there can be no special things.
And there are surely things to be named special.

It is the self's duty to separate.
It is the soul's duty to ease the gap.
And it is spirit that ignites within the spine.
With that gentle awakening becomes
selfless, soulless, formless.

That is god:
limitless potential.
A place of no assumption.

There are layers of tides within the large invisible fishbowl.
God holds holonic systems, without holding.

Hamper

TODAY I WAS FOLDING THE CLOTHES HE LEFT.
They were all empty and clean.
I wished he was in them.

I wished I had the foresight,
to knock the dirty hamper over
and curl up in his scent

before he was
all the way
gone.

Fierce dragons

SCARCITY, FEAR
abrupt change
awakens fierce dragons,
fire-breathers.

Make a sketch or two.
Let your palms know
charcoal and soot
as the heart surrenders
to the contour and scale of
black, white, gray, and light.

One blade makes a clean execution.
Joy in the blood let.
Surely it was tired of running in circles,
circles, circles.
Blood let
for a new breath.

La petite vie

LA PETITE MORT
for every pinnacle,
for every peak.

A little death,
for every border crossed,
for every boundary broken.

Afterward,
the sky cries with me.

Ma petite vie
marked by little deaths,
Little puddles of water by my nightstand.
I marry the bed.
I choose to make up my love
with ghost white sheets.
I wrap them thin around my bare breast
and say my vows
to the solace in lonely ballads,
the comfort in feigning numbness.

The night sky rains stars against my skin
leaving little cigarette burns.
My yellow fingers pry pebbles from my back
for the excavation of craters
that are filled with the emptying
of the ocean's eyes.
I bathe my wounds in little lakes
and reenact *la petite mort*
d'Ophélie.

I drown myself in little lakes.
I know nothing,
except for the way
my life is an earthy-smelling hardback
dog-eared for every peak,
every pinnacle,
every border imagined,
every wall erected,
and their demolition.

I know nothing,
except that
my little life
has been a succession
of little deaths.

Let's play sunshine and moonbelly

LET'S PLAY SUNSHINE AND MOONBELLY.
It starts out with a chase me 'round the earth
and then we'll take turns
glazing each other with brilliant words.

The challenge is calling score,
who is illuminating whom.

I am a character in your dream

I AM THE FREE WOMAN WHO POURS WHISKEY
down her silk blouse,
and allows America to sleep deeply on the inside of
her thigh.
Any citizen who wakes to see my large pale face,
could mistake me for the moon in midday
or would be startled with sleep eyes and a loaded finger,
gargling dry tears in their throat,
saying again and again; angel, demon,

angel, demon, angel demon.

Maintain defense,
it keeps one sheltered.
And shelter is a right.
I hope you never know another thing
you must defend yourself from.
No soul deserves to be raided with shadowy thought.

Poems from New York: I

OFF I GO
into myself,
into my soul,
into what spirit has to say.

Swallow me
without teeth.

Take me
and touch me
in places I may not have been.
Touch me uniquely
in places I have.
Rearrange me
gently.

Listen to my body,
hear my vulnerability
and coax me
into the unknown.

There need not
be too much persuasion.
I would go willingly
to and toward
a thing
that could show me.
Show me.

Show me pleasure.
Show me a loss,

a loss of naivety,
a loss of question.

A filling.
Fill me.
Fill me overflowing.
Let me drink the flowing.

Influence.
Inspiration.

Show me.
Take me.
Touch me
in ways I could not
un-remember.

Poems from New York: II

IS IT THE END OF A CHAPTER?
Are there chapters?

When I make them,
there are chapters,
when I make them.

I can cut my life up like that.
I can understand things like that.

So many run-on sentences.
So many rivers,
lakes, oceans.

So many natural things
used to describe frequent
occurrences.

A thing so ordinary
it marks a coming of age
a block, a pivot, a stone.

A corner turning ...

Poems from New York: III

QUICK, FRONT-ROW STROLL
pass go, collect your drinks.
Must be liquored up
to speak to the little queen
soaring fast and hot
through a red eye night.

Poems from New York: IV

A TALL BEAUTIFUL MAN
reads *Girl, Interrupted*
on the train.

The children's eyes are wide,
not shy.
They stare me down
with an open heart.

I turn away,
afraid
I may show them something
unpleasant.
The city is alive
and full of old dead culture,
entropy
animated
by electricity and business.

Sensitive people
stay home
with their
books, records, and friends
rather than subject themselves
to the tyranny of Manhattan
on a Friday evening.
The DJ spins terrible house,
looping petty thought
as the dancers drink
and drink and drink and dance
and maybe say something to one another,

something about nothing.

There's nothing to be said
in a room full of numbing noise.

The train ride home:
I am spent, disillusioned
and empty feeling.
I want to look up
and find something outside of myself.
I would like to find something within,
but it would only anger me, sadden me
in this place.

Poems from New York: V

THE COMING STORM
brings a morning chill.
I'm rested finally, content.
Exhausted with emotion for Jung.
I am the city that never sleeps.

The city is a lot to hold.
My heart feels small.
I find it easier to love in more open space.

I admire the poets for creating here,
who remained grounded and centered
in this jarring atmosphere.

Poems from New York: VI

SEPARATENESS CREATES STRAIN ON AN EMPATHIC
ability
to understand and transmute certain states of being.
I learn to find darkness in the self and alchemize it.
I come so far from types of fear
that it becomes a long remembering to recognize it in
the other.
A belief persists
even as connective energy becomes more resonant and
palpable.
Boundary dissolves and you are that.
Certainty of oneness is brought forth within you.
As quickly as it is shown it will remove itself from the
seer.

Poems from New York: VII

I WOULD CRY LIKE A NEW CHILD
if I did not know
that I am
and have been held
by a dozen pairs of arms
and one hundred more
coupled eyes and faces.

I have been loved.
I have been loved lustfully
and for all the wrong meanings.

I have been loved
for my anger,
for my fear,
and for my addiction.

I have been loved
for the beauty of being
that I forget too often.

I would wail like a new child
if I believed there was nothing to believe in.

If I could not remember
the times I saw resistance.

If I could not remember
the fierce words I heard randomly
in places I was of custom to muteness.

I would be empty
if the world were not pressing
into my pores every moment
with an urgent message.

The world would be empty
If I would not howl a bit myself.
If I wouldn't fight or fuck.
If I would not love more than I drink.
I would cry like a new child.

I would cry for the first time
when all the places I have learned to be numb
finally relinquish their false control.

I would sing agonizingly then.

Pulse

WHILE HE SLEEPS
his spirit is still.
It is as if he is not there.
Some of his soul is not here.
Thoughts have left
and churn in the belly of all mind.

The breath is steady slow and gently hibernates.
I feel how our lungs and pulse have found rhythmic
resonance.
I gently hold the perspiration of dense gold
that oversees his safe quiet sleep
with all of my breast and belly.
I can taste the way his skin melts in my mouth
when I breathe with my tongue.
How ever simple,
I ask myself,
do I love him?

A small natural child chimes in
with her grand mother,
Venus and Kali,
Lalita and Euterpe, singing
inside of me, singing:
we do, how we do,
yes, we do love him.
dearly
indeed.

Sub-treatise

HOW MANY FEET
shall I sit, stand, lay
away from or around you.

Would you like an anecdote,
a drier sense of humor.
Would you like a dusty quote or two
to wrap a collection
of your unceasing questions in.

Tell me what you like.
How shall I do it.
Is there a way you prefer these types of things to be
performed.
Is there a way you prefer these types of things to be
executed.

If I hold you
where shall I keep my passions,
by the nightstand,
or hidden in the backyard
underneath the grass?

And if I feel
will it scare you.
Will my vulnerability make you flinch.
Will your flinch twist my guts a bit.

How does it feel.
How would you like it.

How many names have you given me.
What do you call me by
when you do not recall the first word
my mother used to describe me.

How many times have you cut me in halves.
How many times could you split me
until I've collapsed
into a chaos more empty than illusion.
You take me in like concepts,
a series of fluid statements
taken through the ears
until your mind is pregnant
and full with contradictions.

You take me in like a dozen kind of medicines,
powdered, pressed, assimilated.
You poison your liver with them
and I leave you with a hunger you cannot feed.
A stomach too empty to fill.
How does it feel.

How shall I present the woman in me.
The nurturer, the womb, the galactic garden.
Are they concepts of matriarchal symbolism
you do not allow yourself to graze your fingers upon.
Has Demeter been,
idolized
taxed
metered
monitored
misconceived.

Is she a pleasure you deny yourself.

Am I pleasure you deny yourself.
How does it feel.

Do you deny the same thing in yourself
that you deny in me.
Am I a hazard to you.
How does it feel.

How shall we assimilate this organic process.
In which ways have you learned to escape what is
in order to protect yourself.
Tell me.

Tell me.
How shall I stylize my performance.
How shall I dance around your fear.
Shall I tiptoe about it.

How does it feel
when I mistakenly walk
into your unmapped darkness.
How shall I do it?

The ever-present kitties

MY KITTENS WERE BORED ONE AFTERNOON.
I left the house for a walk.
When I returned
I found that they had playfully
unraveled all of the yarn.

Every color knotted
in some complex accidental
orchestration.

When there was nothing else
to be done
I sat around and undid
each nest with my fingers
one by one.

I opened the windows wide
and let the lowering winter sun
pour in to dance and lighten my work
amongst all that yarn.

Until the night came
and winter chill fell like snow
upon my freckled skin
as I crocheted a sweater
from the clean balls
I so intricately toiled over.

And the sweater
kept me warm the next winter.

Those without regular names

SHE ISN'T SAYING NO.
She isn't saying yes.
It makes you wonder why
she's here.

She's a silent one mostly
and when you're cruel
you'll get a sneer.

She knows the world's unkind,
and she dreams she could unwind
all the sadness,
all the pain,
the unnecessary dying.

Don't go following her blank stares
you'll find her on a cloud
where she's one with
smoke and mirrors,
vast emptiness,
and doubt.

Let her be when her eyes are welling.
There's not a word that could describe,

how the world could be so fine
if she weren't young as a seed,
more old than time.

Very human

VERY HUMAN
as I suspected
and a little like me.

Preaching limitless,
spinning the thought out of mouth
through ears and round and round in mind
trying it against the boundary of ego.
Human turned sublimate, hovers over
so that it stands still,
still stands before the aspects.

Interaction,
a damn that pulls the waters of flaw and flawless
passions, tumultuous
within a container made of fear.

Consistently floating above it all
laughing and going,
look what a foolish thing!

Just above it
and then spirit gets tired.
Finding self embodied
waist deep in the earth, the mud, the tides.
Little lakes filled with mythical sea things.

Fear, pain, addiction, human, mammalian, reptilian
dimensions sickened with spite and ignorant authority.

An elite spirit more ego-like than absolving.

Still, still using the body
the continuous tool of flesh, palms, knuckles, and knees.

Torn and torn childish fit raging, raging,
the thought, limitless, spins and spins
as concept
unscathed disintegrates into a piece of pieces,
limitless limited
and held from the physical world like a relic.

Forged in tongues of eel.
Eel of human fear.
Eel locked away in the sentient body
of little crevices disowned by itself.

Wringing

ARRIVE AND DO SILENT WORK.
Go when the monsters come.

The candle is too easily engulfed
by darkness.

One wolf howls in the night
and out goes the light.

Sweet young thing,
they want your joy.
They are going to eat your heart,
little one.

It's a narrow path to hell
they're going to
squeeze you in too.

There's no point warring in darkness.
Best to go, do silent work.
Wait until the stars are aligned
to rise.

Sleep, until you are awakened,
by the call of ascension.

A moment when all hearts
sing in the same key.
One long ringing.
One long marriage.

A snail fell

A SNAIL FELL ON THE CEMENT.
It made a cracking sound.

As I picked her up,
I was worried her shell
may have fractured
from the two story fall.

I picked her up gently
and placed her on the garden bed.
The soil was dark and moist.

I told her to sleep and rest well.

Abstractions of prosperity

ELEGANT PIMPS.
Masters of their dynasties.

Tell them what they would like to hear.

Leave out the parts
that paint
a sad face.

No one mistakes you
for the sun
or the moon,
darling.
It's too clear
we all want more.

Stick to "I" statements
and positive reinforcement.

Absurd good news

I'VE GOT A LONG WAY TO GO.
When paths cross,
their eternities collapse.
A cosmic spiral dance, in.
A cosmic spiral dance, out.
We are dirty and silent
upon release,
and we are not free,
until we forget.
As I climb up from an unconscious dance,
I forget to breathe.
I feel so long underwater.
I've got a half-gill in my right rib.
Poems in my heart die,
as I gasp for air.
Here on shore,
where I am not truly sure of
anything.

Imagination!
You fool!
I won't trust you.
Imagination.
You are no longer a part of me.
Come back, when you do not grab
at my heart's childish desire!
You make me a sane man.
So that I cannot be free.

All and is

WE LEAVE TO WRITE THE POEMS
and play the songs
that were stuck in our souls.

Knowing they were there.
Feeling them churning.

Letters, from every alphabet.

A warm soup,
that was no comfort
in the bowl, in the mouth,
or on the floor.
Something must be done!
Something had to be made!

The sound of it hummed
in her body,
with no reference.

Another language?
A new way to make love?

How will all finally be
expressed as it is.

Ananda

MY DREAMS SLIPPED AWAY.
I dream so many things.
Even my daydreams are frequent.

They bubble up
show me truths, and
dissipate!

They go.

No words, not even a picture.
Just a haunted feeling, with
a crumb of wisdom in it.

A wisdom,
I am tortured to seek.

If I could eat this one morsel
it would calm all of my senses.
It would be the one taste.
One taste for all of the tastes.

One taste,
could get boring, I say.
Today,
there will be love,
like no other.

I have been feeling this love,
rise within me.
It soars.

It glides.
It is beauty, god, ecstasy.
I wanted to call this feeling,
man.
I wanted to call it,
anything.

I am almost certain now
that it is the sky.
The galaxies.
A sound ringing
through all things.

So base it is
no longer heard.

Archer and eclipse

NO LINES
no bows
no arrows
to raise.

I am suspended.
I am humming.
My stomach is the lining
of nothing, nothing.

I am lost,
floating.
I make.

I wait,
until my pain
has no language.
Until,
I cannot say
a name.

Until my pain
is not even an "I".

I want an empty heart.
I want a space
that holds nothing.
A space so grand,
it merely echoes back
an exact sound,
a ringing like that.

A booming. A thing,
that does not change.
An unconditional softness,
soft as a breeze is.

Hot like my skin.
Not human,
something more.

My body,
is not a cage.
It is not a house.
It is not a cave.

I am light,
and it will be so.
It is so.

I forget too easily,
I believe that "I am".
That I am sane, or insane.
That I am—moon or sun.
That I am—anything.

Bottom

WE LEARN FROM BOTTOM.
That's where the good stuff is.

Fishing shiny pebbles from the mud.

I still go out and walk.
I speak in spurts.
I find there's rarely anything to say.
It is rare that there is not a hard thing to say.

Life rolls on.
I go with it.
In silence there is gnosis.
The repetitive tape forever plays.

The beat goes on.
The record spins.

Boys I

FOR THOSE THAT LOVE THEIR LEADERS
who bring god in to tame them.
Who find themselves righteous.

Who quote Nietzsche, and are
ambivalent toward their mothers.

Boys II

THE BOYS ARE UPSTAIRS
imitating their fathers.

One is growling deeply.
I can almost see his teeth dripping,
as the other shows a funny stoned smile.

Playing still.
Letting wrath show itself.

Cartel

THE MORNING COFFEE
means nothing anymore.
I sip it half-heartedly.
I do not know the time.

03022013

A WHOLE SLIPPING
a jump, a flight
we've no recollection of taking.
The sweetest love comes this way.
With the silencing of chatter,
in a total surrender.

If we were to unravel
all that would be is vastness.
A pitch-black room.
A place to feel through.

Best hold the fear of mystery.
Hold the theory that
keeps essence from becoming.

I wish that I were not bound
by preference and history.
That I did not recall.
Not a face, or a name for myself.

5. Venus in the Seventh

06182013

For Anne Sexton and Adrienne Rich

I HAVE DISCOVERED HER
her worry, her marble grief
printed over, dispensed
in black and white.

I run my fingers through the tar
of her evenings.
The marks I leave on her coffee mugs
are the pieces I long-begged of the muses.

I may not pluck a string again.
I may not exit my front door.
Density has found me.
I touch her words,
solid,
true.

More tangible than little ripples spoken,
whispers tremble through puddles.
Pebbles skipped across the drought of
earth.
Bridges built over empty reservoir.

I have found her
disclosing honest nightmares.
She leaves them scattered about the house,
little scraps of paper litter the bookshelves, the ashtrays.

Photographs capture her in stillness.

Her smirk, her wrists, the whites around her pupils.
The pressed linen dress.
Her thin thigh rests atop her pink knee.

A few frames, hardly convey her poetry.
The ridicule,
the depth, the wit,
and poise of her language.

Guadalupe

LAST NIGHT AS I WAS DREAMING
I saw Guadalupe.
She was gorgeous and vibrant.
Her hair, long and thick, dark.

She was from deep in the Amazon.
Her skin the softest dew,
tough from sun.
Bronze, gold, and luminous she was!

She wore a head covering
the colors of red, magenta, and orange.
The colors of red desert mountains.
Her lips, bubblegum pink.
I wanted to kiss her.
My mouth trembled.

Around her body,
was turquoise and jade,
the colors of algæ on spring rocks.

She glanced at me once,
to make sure I knew who she was.

A light being in a long robe
came to my right side.
Their face was dark beneath their hood.

They came quickly,
then retreated.
They touched me softly,

with a blackness that was cool,
robbing Guadalupe's warmth from me.

Hot lady

MADNESS UNHINGES A BIT.
My inner world a fountain of pages,
loaded lines alluding to history ...
a man who fearlessly spews
his unconscious on a field
of open-eared hearts
with the courage to know
that he would not harm them
with his power ...
I have kept a tally of each thought.
I have thrown the old inventory away.
I labeled the junk letters obvious
primary fliers, prescribing
more sex,
more will,
more power,
more food,
more taste.
Too many tastes,
too much fire.

My will is the last push over the cliff,
offering the most holy sacrifice.
I eat air, caffeine,
nicotine, and the occasional vegetable.
I tread lightly.

Allow me the eccentric.
It is my last frontier.
Limitlessness,
I found once in a child's daydream.

The child's daydream said,
that the world simply needed
more play, more wonder,
and lighthearted work.

As a young woman I say,
we need to pull the other galaxies down here,
to whisper our futures in our ears.
As a mother I say, be gentle with them.
As a lover I say, there is time for wrath.

I traded my ear worms in for worm holes.
I set rhythmic fires on my front lawn
and offer the ashes of my transgression
as a thick cleansing scent to my relatives.

If you see me,
be certain that I know you are sentient.
All is forgiven in the heart of a woman
who has forever been casting herself
into shadows.

I can't wear your boxers anymore

I CANT WEAR
your boxers
anymore.

I hope I'm making you uncomfortable

I HOPE I'M MAKING YOU UNCOMFORTABLE
because, I'm making myself uncomfortable.

I keep looking in the fridge

I KEEP LOOKING IN THE FRIDGE
and he's not in there.

I miss you

I CHECK THE STARS
then I check on you ...
I imagine what you are working on.
I imagine you are well.
I imagine you are strong.
And I miss you.

Maia

SHE HOLDS THE NUANCE OF HER SURROUNDINGS
She is space, space to be filled.

Allowed. With acknowledgment and choice.

She holds every story that has ever touched her.
She holds the galaxy in her spine:

The water of life in her pleasure,
sustenance of eternity,
in her breast.

She bleeds her joy out,
red and brown,
as the earth.

Meursault

TELL ME MORE OF MEURSAULT, MY DARLING ONE
I have heard of your work, piling up, up, up
over your beautiful crown.

My queen, my lady of the sweetest bouquet,
I long to read your essays.

I am afraid I may not understand.
Could you smile for me as you pass them here?

I may take them home, and cry,
cry for the wisdom you create,
water them with my heart, so that they can grow.
Grow us all a softer earth.

I tend the ground this way, here.
As I trust you are there,
making the way it will all be.

How I believe in you ...

Nice dream

SOMETIMES WE HAVE BAD DREAMS
when we are awake.

Sometimes we have bad dreams
when we are asleep.

Either way there will be good dreams
and there will be bad dreams.

No-span

FOR ALL THE BEAUTIFUL WORDS
we could not speak:
I am not sure how they come to be.

Tell me.
All I hear are longings.
I hear the trauma in you.
I hear the way your
inner child howls in darkness.

For simple reasons.
Simple reasons,
that at most moments
one does not care
to give meaning ...

Meaning,
search out
that new outrage on the
no-span channel.

"I do not want to write *Howl* again".

I want to write forgiveness.
I write forgiveness on everything.

On the sad face,
the awkward jerk;
the drunkenness of friends.
I love them, surely
I love them.

Yet, when I am alone on a rainy day,
I am reminded of the pain we were hiding.

The pain, that pain.
Some do well to manage it.
Over seize,
disillusioned,
autonomous, free.
Free to chain myself to anything,

Box myself in.
Insert self, here › (   )

One-thousand upheavals.
Child who embraces destruction.

Loving the scars and shrapnel.

Shrapnel is confetti.

Balloons are filled with
lungs, lungs, lungs,
then collapse.

The exposing of breast.
The explosion of chests.

Overlapping,
folding, folding
into itself
and then out.
Never flat.
Never straight.
Never clean.

Wrinkled love
made material.
Forever wrinkled sheets.

Pierceson

THE HERO RETURNS WITH MEDICINE FOR THE TRIBE.
Their award is intimate devotion.

Rise and confine

AS SOON AS I WAKE
the cartography begins
pressing itself into my reality.
Confining me in its tiny boxes.
Gifting me to myself.
Taking me away,
and giving me back
in its own words.

Please, do not
shove my being back at myself.
Let me breathe.
I've got
open wounds, a sore throat,
a sore pelvis,
and a sore heart.

If you won't hold me gently
and speak in questions,
leave me being.

If I had only listened
to what my intuition said,
I would have found my home by now.

I shut her up and off sometimes,
and go round in circles
more than twice ...

I want a clean structure,
that won't cut me up

into cubes,
a connective grid
invisible to the sane eye.

Romantic dogs

CHASTITY BELLS
ringing.
Mad as dogs.
Where did the dogs come from?
They're playing hopscotch in the weeds.
The weeds are under the sea.
Romantic dogs.

Science and accidia

ACCEPTANCE OF ENTROPY
and decline.

A back slope,
myopia,
clout in the eyes.

Fight, flight,
or freeze.

Fake,
steel, fear
and shine.

Rise in the morning,
sink
back
down.

Submerging
a candle in the bathtub.

Seek silence

NOT AN EXTRA SOUND.
Only the water,
and the buoy.
I reflect upon harsh wind,
fast speeches,
anxiety.

Presence
discovers simple sweetness.

I drink alone,
and tell traveling men to seek silence.

Shakespeare's sister

SHAKESPEARE IS MY BROTHER.
We have been born
on the same day.
We are Taurus together.

I am his lost sister.
I tend to tiny hot stars
in the vastness of earth's
wondering eyes.

Who knows how Shakespeare
could write of love as he did?

I do.

I know because,
we are plainly related.

He wrote for Pleiades.
He wrote for the constellation
born above his hand.

He witnessed their budding light
which brought tears to his eyes.
Which watered and tickled his bare toes.
Which brought ink into his pen.
He took love from them, as I do.
As I take love from him
and give it back—to you.

Who knows how Shakespeare

could write of love as he had?

I do.

Shark ray at Crystal Pier

I WENT TO THE BEACH.
We were on the pier.
We had a blanket.
I still have the blanket.

The men were fishing.
They caught a little shark ray.
He was flipping and sad.

I took them from the fishing men.
I wrapped them in the blanket.
I walked fast back down the pier
and around to the edge of the ocean.

I set them down under the waves.
The waves pulled him in.

BJ said, they would just die and get beached.
I never talked to BJ again.

Sit

SIT
and the teacher and student
come at once.

Symphony 92

ASSIST THE ALCHEMY OF SORROWS,
with a fierce love.
A courageous love,
that sees and admires the potential
in those that may not recognize
their own strength.

Your clear resonance with others,
will sing a song that
would move the strings,
of any orchestra,
toward symphony.

Synesthesia

TELL THE YELLOW SOUND TO BE SILENT!
I don't like the sun
shining through the dashboard
this afternoon.

Perhaps, a blue sound ...
A purple note ...
Red ink etchings,
on the drums of my ears.

An invisible mollusk ...
A floating sheer sea creature,
deep within a mysterious womb.

Who meets all of the magic
I speak with.
In, on, off
of trances.

The myth of power

BE CAREFUL WHAT YOU WISH FOR
when you show the world
you long to die long enough,
it will eat you.

It is not about
fighting to stay up.
It is not struggle.

If you find life a struggle,
then you will always be tired.
You will always be heavy.

And when you lie down,
for that long,
you can very easily be swallowed,
by the earth.

Contemplate gratitude,
even when exhausted.
Be happy to know,
you did enough.
Enough of all you were called to do.

Do not let anyone tell you
that you are living for them.
Never mistakenly struggle for power.
There is no struggle for power.

Waiting on the bull

THE MYSTERY
and wonder
of a woman's womb

how she bleeds.
How she allows release.

I love to stay home
and wait on her.
To feel her
freely filling in my hips.

Oh mother, your blood
flows from my being.

I am gentle as the bull.

Vehicle of boundless balance

FIGHTING THE PARTY DEMONS
until the wild cows come home.

I'm in a range of fire.
Freedom is clocked out,
immaculate barbed wire.

Rapunzel hangs herself
from a fifty-foot building
in London.

She was such a pretty virgin,
until her face turned into
a blue smile.

I always loved the feeling
of falling, falling
falling
      falling
            falling
                  of falling ...

It does not end.

I have not died yet again.
Just yesterday
I was clearly Christ,
my heart the true goddess,
my body Merkabah.

I saw with x-ray halo vision,
my ex-lover's blessing.

It trickled
down
the crown of my head,
yolk and all.

And nearly made it
all
the way,
down
      down
            down
                      down, toward my hips

My hips have teeth now.
They have teeth now.

My vaginal walls,
tighten more and more
and more,
with every sound
of a ruffling muscle.

I am safety.
I am skin ... I am mortal, again.

Again, again,
tell me how have I forgotten eternity.
I forget five times before breakfast.
I go off on holiday with ego, my good friend.

While the soul festered in some distant
metaphysical textbook.

I have no appetite.

The car's driving.
It's got some parts
I don't understand.

You're driving it ... I'm driving it
neither of us know,
which is which.

I call myself
a rainbow black flag
I wave as soon as someone throws
the first brick:
I'm getting all of my money back.
I was poking holes in the grain vat.

06182013ii

HEAVY LIMBS LOWER
taking rest.

She returns to the earth,
marries her.
Once she went as embers
burnt by the flames of her own passion.

Today she goes down easy.
Her glistening skin speaks shrilly in aloneness.
She breathes slow with silence.
Her thin arms tremble with each turn of the shovel.

There is no audience.
Nothing conveys shock or notion of suffering
as she lowers herself into bed.

She goes to Gaia willingly.
She gives herself safely to the womb.

To learn of patience.
To be sedentary.
She bears no weight,
but the true density of matter.

11112013:1:21pm

THIS IS HOW A WOMAN BECOMES FREE.
She becomes so empty of illusion
that her sadness no longer wears a face.
Her comforts are inanimate,
a hot whiskey, a nicotine fix.

She decides there is nothing more beautiful
than her bare breasts in the winter.
There is no love as strong
as the love that lets her body shake and sob
and shiver during the sleep of a city,
where not a soul can hear her childish dreams breaking.

There is no greater sex
than the love she makes with herself
when she runs her fingers through her unshowered hair,
or roughly tugs a comb through its nests.

A woman is free
once she learns to love her grief so well
she finally
allows its release,
then tends to nothing in emptiness.
Her god is nothing as well.
She can sleep with her face in a damp pillow case
and want nothing
but the taste of her own salt
and the wet of all of her own pleasure and pain.

She can get dirty with that.
She can clean herself up with that.

She would not long for purity then.

She would be a swamp and a lithium spring,
diamond and rock,
the same.
In her own sweet embrace.
In her own bed,
that she could call a home
or do without.

Then she could come and go without a name.

Without a mirror.
With a song only made of consonants.
A love without continents.
A longing too long unrequited.
A static raw beam.
An ivory pillar of eternity.

A sort of exit

NOTHING WOULD FILL MY HUNGER FOR BLISS
but a break,
a true fracture.

I sought god,
I found my spine
and was sent to speak with darkness,
in a sterile waiting room.

A chrome hell.
A new sort of purgatory.
Doors guarded by sets of perfect piercing ivory.
One may always pull them from their hinges.

An exit!
A fast play!
A clever chattering skeletal specimen.

A rant.
A wish.
A lot of hot air.

Anahata

HEART FALLS OPEN
instantaneously.
A tomb beaming light.

I am not sure what's in there.
Its fierce-with-fear eyes.
Closer to eternity from the sky.

Heart sings a heavy tone
of each octave.
Lifting every object in the room.
Shaking it around,
naming it a word that it forgets,
and then sets them gently down.

There were some moments
we did not ask for our eyes to see
perfection.

Every object the same.
Every object a bow
that rings against the strings of
heart's innumerable cords.

Voices ring in here.
In here / out there.
I have practiced for this moment.
I have practiced
lucidity, acceptance.

The moment multiplies by itself.

Faster than a large machine.
The moment has no increment.

I have followed heart into
swamps, caves, total desolation.
Heart has been silenced by
a cigarette, confusion.

I have dreamt of a room that could glow.
Shine in the perfect lightness.
When all the shadows and grayscales become
vibrant color.

I have forgotten forever.

The memory of heart
lifts me right out of myself
with the pure joy of an unconditional child.

With eyes too bright to see.
Vast as so many galaxies.
Bright as all of our suns.
Deep as psychic wombs
wounds, and so many oceans.

In heart's space
the beautiful and ugly hold each other
in tearful union
then begin to chuckle and laugh
ecstatically.
Angels visit here,
people with crystal lights
beaming from their pores.

Their wholeness sings infinities
and strikes me.

I allow a resonance.
A resonance, ringing out
with all of it
us, them, we

Brother

I'VE NOT WRITTEN IN MONTHS.
I'm tossing a few words into the collection plate tonight,
coins into the welling of your throat
as half-a-fifth of rum makes its way into the gutter in
your cul-de-sac.

Late wishes to patch up the roof of the mansion of art
we'd made together.
An old dilapidated frame that coughs ghostly stanzas.
The steps croon minor chords under quiet feet.

Its damn near freezing underneath this dark sky.
Tomorrow we wake to alarm clocks
and scrub teeth we won't show under fluorescence.

You used to love to play the blues.
Now the guitar just sits in the corner
its strings fall out of tune.

Somewhere in last five years we've grown to realize
the soaring heart of one privileged suburbanite
cannot demolish the decades of cement laid over the
natural earth.

Rage feels a lot like power
until you fall asleep with it in your chest one night
and wake up with a torn throat.
Voice is out for a week.

Power makes its home abroad,
the effects look like third world countries

and global warming propaganda,
the new agers name fear, and ignore.

I'm not sure what you are seeing,
I thought maybe I could write something
that bent the images in all your photographs.

Maybe I could say something that put an end to all of this ...

something that could put the light back in your eyes.
Something that could keep you from turning every
single light out.

Like maybe,
the bird perched on that tree in your courtyard,
will fly toward the coast and breathe the salty air
that used to leave you wet some mornings,
when you were homeless by the ocean.
Or maybe, your hands are birds that comb the salt in a coming lover's hair
as she lays drying under the sun in your lap.
And the guitar is whispering to you from the corner.
its strings now at a perfect drop D.

And you never heard the first person that asked you to second-guess your passion:
or the second, or the third.
In fact, no one ever asked you to rethink your passion at all.
No one would dream of it.
They let you be a dreaming man in love with six strings and the sea.
"God's eyes are crossed, just like yours".

Crow

CROW MAKES A PASS AT WISDOM,
they like to slip rocks into my pocket,
as I stride below their one good eye.

Their feathers taunt me,
mangled as the hobos
that share morning coffee in
silent enlightenment.

Crow says,
watch for meteors
streaking invisible in midday.
This town is not as it seems.
The hot anger I gift you with,
is the red pin you must be ready to
slide through the heart of beasts.
Know beasts, you are one.

Crow says,
from up here, you are all comfortably,
silently padding through the ruins of Greece.

I have taken the sandpaper portal
from branch to branch,
compromised my good look.
See how the ivory bones
of my vessel corset
remind one of impermanence?

The rock is not a thing you understand.
You have not been pressed so long.

You have not worn yourself out.
You do not know exposition.

Young thing, you're hot as lead.
You're the making of steel,
volcanic eruption.

You know no annual geyser,
no purity.

You do not know leap year.
Your speech,
whipped cream aerosol.
too sweet,
too white.
Just like new.

Pomegranate

I WANT TO PICK THE UNRIPE FRUIT.
I want to crack the thick skin
and let the bitterness hang in between my teeth.
I may tongue and drink that dry substance.
I salivate for the deception of my own creation.
And call his sweat the sweetest thing
I have ever tasted.

For my lover, returning

I AM ELATED,
lemon zest and citrus
the season provides
for my weak defenses.

I am ecstasy.
My lover returns
in three months, this moment.

My lover, returns
again and again

each time,
the sun touches
my winter skin.

God has given us our blessing.
God has given him our blessing.

Blessings, suspended
in the brilliance of
perfect nest of light.

I am on holiday,
all afternoon.

I am drunk,
with eternal love.

I have not cut

IF I WERE TO CHOOSE A SONG TO WRITE EACH EVENING
I would write of falling in love, a never-dying.
And I would not wonder
how I was convinced we could cut
something apart.

I have not cut.
I write the names of lovers between each line.

It will do

MAN OF LAW AND MEDITATIONS OF EARLY WAR.
He asks only for the lingering bouquet of
woman left in his sheets.

He says, I love the scent of collected kindling,
from around my father's cabin.
And this will do.

Upon waking he re-enters the room
and holds her body, back to belly.
A paperweight,
before she's scattered her selves across the dawn.

Leave the scent, he said,
it will do.

The fruit that ate itself

WHEN THE ANGER COMES MY RIBCAGE SHUDDERS.
My heart bruises its selves.

It says, I'm getting old now.
We're all going to self destruct in 5...3...1...7...

Erratic sequences
play my bones.
I am a xylophone.
I forget language.
I do not know the word, anger.
I know force.
Force melts my mind.
My heart an old fruit no one will eat.

Could you hold something like that?
Could something hold
the destruction of eternity's beliefs
collapsing into the one body?

When you shudder.
I want to eat your heart before it spoils.
I want to dive quickly across the room
and save its sweetness with my mouth.

Before another peace can perish
in the hard earth
that grows hotter and hotter
beneath our feet.

Everything is—shaking.

Everything is ringing
with the madness
that longs to expose itself.

To be seen with present audience.
To not go falling,
rolling, scurrying off
to rot in the corner.

A ghost of fertile rage
hidden behind a curtain,
and an ocean,
and a cloud of illegible ink.

Remnants of Inanna in winter (I–XI)

I

AND HE HIDES HIS SECRET DREAMS.
He tells me again that I am not ready,
that he is not ready.
He turns from me,
down another winding path.
I know nothing of him.

I know nothing but his soul, his beautiful soul.
The silent stillness of his heart
that once called to me in sleep,
with no ruler, no name, with a kind of warmth.

I could not let him leave me.
For this my heart truly cries.
My heart cries. My heart cries. My eyes cry.
My chest is concave.
My body pulls into itself,
retracts, and says it never wants another thing.
No other man.

Please, please.
I cannot think I am not intelligent.
I cannot believe that I am not love.
I must be treated as such.
Remembered as such.
I cannot bear the hatred.
I cannot bear the breath that slows.
The breath, that dies in my chest.
The sadness creeping in.

The silent dying.
The little war.
The little war.

II

HE IS NOT HERE ANY LONGER.
I cannot pine for him truly.
Though I did pine when he was with me.
When he was with me
I could not place my head on his chest.
He could not love me.

He has divorced me.
Had another woman come to say,
that he could never be mine.

How terrible.
How wretched it is
to never be loved.

To be told that I am not enough.
That I cannot be used for what I am.
That I have not earned ...

III

AH, BUT LET HIM DREAM.
Let him dream.
Please, let him dream.
Dream himself awake from this terrible state
of never allowing beauty into his body.

IV

AM I SELFISH FOR WONDERING
whether he is wounded?
Am I selfish, for wondering:
would he have me if I were better,
if I were different?

I know I allowed the love.
And still ... he said he could not love me.
He could not take me.
He could not have me.

Was it the heroin?
Was it the drugs?
Was it the fear?
Was it the waiting to be taken by his angels?

I almost believe he wanted to die.
He lived in other worlds.
He was gone most of the time.
He could not be coaxed from a place where angels lived.
Angels, who are gorgeous.

V

HOW SAD, FOR A MAN
not able to admit true love.
A love, that wraps his body up in
warmth, desire,
and compassion.

VI

I GIVE POWER TO HIM BY WRITING THIS.

I must submit.

If I fear pain,
I fear the whole of existence.
I fear the whole of being.
The whole of my being knows fear.
I have been courageous.
I have fought.
I have been vulnerable.
Truly, I am only happy when I am vulnerable.
I want to be pink.
Pink, pink.
Again!
I want my glowing heart to be a true thing.
A true light.
Let me breathe. Please.

VII

ALL THAT I DESIRE IS DESIRE.
Desire.

Heart,
awaken again.

Soul, you are a fool.
You have seen your own brilliance.

Forgive projection.

Forgive separation.
Forgive.

I want to forgive him.
I am not ready.

My soul is not happy that it has lost her ...
My soul is devastated that is has lost her.
Lost, him. Lost the cosmic depths.

VIII

WATER, WAKE UP.

Take my body.
Take me, take me.
Take me down the river.

Take me down.
Like a twig,
I would leave my home,
to feel caught,
to feel passions again.

I would fall from the tree,
A perfect auburn leaf.

It is still fall in this city.
It is still fall in this place
where the seasons are warmer.

All sweats more than before.
Must I wait another season to know

that I am always all seasons.

I am always all seasons.

IX

I DO NOT KNOW THE THINGS IN BOOKS.
My body is temple.
Body, the shrine.
Body, the cup, the vessel.
The all thing.
The one taste.
The one sight.
The one breath.
Fire does not purify this.
I need water to be cleansed,
and long for the ocean.

I long for the ocean.
La mar, return to me.
La mar, my love.
My goddess.
I have missed you dearly.
I long for your wrath,
your turning in my belly.

Her womb. Forever.
Ocean and galaxies.
I look up to find the mother in me.

The men must know Aphrodite.

I cannot become so hard.

Softness, water is softness as water is ...

Oh mother, cleanse me.
Oh mother. Cleanse me.
I call upon the goddess.

The goddess, she must be here somewhere ...
Let me be the earth.
Let me be the ocean.
Let me be the breath in the trees,
birds in the sky.
Let me be those things.

I have become too serious always.
And for this I apologize.
Please forgive me.
I forgive you.
I thank you. I love you.

x

I HOLD TOO LONG.
I hold him too long.
I hold the past too long.
I hold the future too long.

I am grateful for this breath, here.
I am grateful for the pouring of words.
I am thankful for these things.
I have no other utterance but gratitude.

Imagination, thank you.
I allow you to distract me from the womb.

XI

LET ME HAVE HER.
Let me have my body.
Let me have my pain.
Let me have my truth.
Let me have the water.
Let me have the earth, back.

Let me have her.
I am coming to take her back.
I am coming to retrieve the goddess from you.

She has always been mine to weep inside of.
She has always been mine.
If a man can call her out.
He is great. No matter if he tends to fear her.
No matter if he tends to revoke his warmth, his sun,
his embrace.

I long for the beauty of man.
I long to feel the power in him,
the softness of him.
I am bitter too long.
I tell my heart to be too silent.
Beauty return to me.

Lover. Return.
In any form.
You must return.

Walls are erected to hide from the state.
I do not even trust myself with my own love.
I fear to be a sap.

I fear to melt into the softness.

Let me have her. Let me take her.
She is mine. She has always been.
She was before the pain and sadness.

She was a glowing child that I forget.

The best parts of art

THIS IS MODERN POETRY.

There is no meter,
nor notation.
No metric,
no rhythm.

Who is to blame
but the self.
The self-denying god?
The mind?
Separating so often
it no longer grasps?

There are so many songs
of love we can write.

There is so much we can do
with twoness:
blame,
trade,
force,
union.

"The best parts of any works of art,
Are the beginnings and the ends".

The curious call

HOW TO SAY,
I feel nothing,
until you enter my space.

I dreamed too fondly,
held you in every drawer,
in the mind,
in my ribs.

I rolled you over,
the living room,
the kitchen,
my heart's floor.
I never let you leave.
When you are here,
I am full.
It is energy,
astral,
causal,
celestial.

Your songs are overlapping.
The faces intertwine.
Lovers before.
Lovers during.
After.
In the midst of every face that
weaves through folktale,
I hear you are lying with me
in orange blossoms,
and white tea.

And I hear myself, a sullen girl
wide awake in your bed
while you sleep heavily.

I teethe the bitter pomegranate
I find each spring.

I have left many poems and sketches
in galleries, lovers float through.

You have finally met my father
and I have burned you both,
in the fires of summers coming,
summers gone.
I hear your tremolo subtly sending
the curious call to your wife.
She sleeps peacefully,
her son's face looms with your histories
and tenderness.

A set of slurs for you, my dear.
A howling moon,
an island of beauty
once strung and tuned too.

I was a stanza rewritten
with endless eyes and pores for your night.
I was more than constellation.
I echoed through rooms you made with fingers
soft upon the freights
that held dreams,
trading good stillness.

Flash flood on California Top 20 (R)

SCANNING SCATTERED RANTING
at the bottom of a coffee cup.
Constellations dried,
swamp stencil, seaside.

One blank journal
I'm not willing to hide.
Lines are gray
A place to hold, Abraxas,
a division of color
seen through the eyes
of a mere animal.
I'm left with
one hundred years of solitude.
It checked out
after three transgressing "shoulds".

I never read the books they told me to.
I remained on the surface.
Allowing the madness of passions
to eat my pen.

A stomach full of bourbon
one summer,
when you were in love
with piss creole brick.
A stomach full of Greyhounds
and kerosene vodka,
the spring you said,
the bitter pomegranate in my gums
was product of insomniatic sleepwalk.

Stop.
A mouth full of sandbag cheeks
grinding down my wisdom teeth.
I can write from pain,
when I pretend you are holding me.
He let me live on clouds when I was ten.
When I was five,
I saw angels
drifting across the desert skyscape.
Animals were born,
prominent as dinosaurs.

It's worth the word
when it's written.
Any other time, it's a static channel,
fucking with the receptionist,
whose morning hangover makes her deaf
to your sarcasm.

I'm left to ponder lineage of man.
My father. His father. Your father.
Mind obstinate. A nun.

I am sure of my skull these days.
I am sure it is, here, electric.
It won't let the doe-eyed animals through
to wave a frail
hello.
I call this panic.
I call you theory.
Theory and myth.
I haven't got the prophecy.

I read him clearly.

Long enough.
I read a chattering mouth of plastic teeth.
Tapping fingers on a lock-jaw typewriter.
Saying: Yes. No. Maybe.
Let me. I want. Go away.
Save me.
Mom. Sister. Kitten.
You're wet. Brush your teeth.
Shave your face.

I was a nightstand. Pillowcase.
Lamp. Rug. Coffee mug.
Inanimate, surely.
Wash. Rinse. Wring. Repeat.

There is a rhythm in uncertainty.
There is a rhythm in release.

I hear my neighbor tapping madly in his hot garage.
As his wife collects worms from around the flowering broccoli.

"We got hot and died".

I use my drumsticks as chopsticks.
We fuck for natural laxative.

Take up punk living room dancing, Arizona, in June.
Smear the glitter from an androgyne's chest
on your cheeks.
Have an ice cube. No need for explanation.
The songs were made, and made, again.
The only thing that gets us out of this room
is the photographer's waterbed.

I wasn't there
the time you played that song, you wrote,
about the time, I snuck in through your back door,
and fell asleep with your extra pillow.
Young hands full of gin and cranberries,
jazz guitar and body.
I wasn't listening when you said,
I was the wildest thing you ever did.
I wasn't listening when you said,
you would never do that again.

I didn't listen to Townes Van Zandt.
I never got around to *Tropic of Cancer*,
because, I believed, you and I
were the true erotic piece.

I only wrote the heartbreak.
I never said ... I never said,
you were beautiful to me.

I was drinking up on *Cold Mountain*.
I was reading *Brave New World*.
I was reading *Anarchy A–Z*.
I said, take this as homework.
You said, I only speak Business Degree.
I only speak: Brophy, jazz, and your body.

I was sipping fresh citrus
in backyard jungle hammocks,
made by a mother church, and *Star Treck* DVDs.
I lost my top, flipped over a fence, and fell on a baby stroller.
I started a garden you never planted a seed in.
I forgave god.

I lucid dreamed.
You weren't there.

I showed you tantric videos.
You ate the first bowl of soup I ever made.
We scrawled ourselves all over my new legal pad,
fell asleep, and you left before I awoke.
It was kind of you.
Hello, good morning, goodbye:
is three glances.
Leave it at one,
and no one is held,
or accountable.

Only we could do these things.
Only we could play time this way.
Only we could say no so strongly.

Obstinate, as a tree perched in snow.
A lightswitch that wouldn't flip.
A door that would not open.
You weren't there. I'm not sorry.

Forgiveness isn't a verb.
It's a stanza, pinned and needled
on my inner arm.
It's a stanza,
until we make it a song.
Forgiveness, it's religious.
There's no such thing.

I was your real thing.
Your Zen nun.
We played backwards practice.

No rule books.

I let you squeeze me until I turned blue.

It's worth the word when it's written,
I could write a record about you.
It's a stanza, until we add sound.

The sound of tiny work

AND FOR THE PITTER-PATTER OF DELICATE FINGERS
on surfaces solid, and misinterpreted.

There is nothing
except the rhythm discovered
in such a moment,
when inspiration floods the body.

Nothing as mystical
as a song of delicate tapping.
As droplets of water arriving
on my window pane.
As June bugs zip into the second-story screen.

Sounds of tiny fingers.
Sounds of tiny insects.
Sounds of tiny work.

Tonight I can write, as Neruda

I DREAMED OF RIDING
a twin blow-up bed as a raft
down the canal.

The water ran fast
and took my sorrows
with its rippling.

I sang of the burning in my belly.
The burning that tickled
my shriveled heart,
until my heart throbbed.

A cool wind
kissed the skin on the back of my neck,

one thousand times.
I was awakened to my sorrow.

You're the type of person that I'll be looking for

I TRIED HIM OUT
and in that way
we were bound a bit.

Bound by the kittens
who took the lives we shared.

I read his perforated braille
which tracked packs of chimps
escaped from pen.

I could have been a woman
up in a tree
protesting the Pope's reassignment.

I came up from a basement
filled with dull opiate static.
Young men were turning up gain to blow tubes.

Came down from his stories of Ana.
Ana, the way her name fluttered in our hearts.
Ana, a love that stuck.

Still, a name can take new form
each time it is spoken.

I told him I was watercolor,
crying on a guitar I could not
play or purchase.

He said, chin up,

be glad you're not drowning in Memphis.

He wrapped my ascetic corpse in poetry,
showing me tongues of forgotten ancestors,
squatting in field, delivering seed to hollow.
He was waiting out the delivery of his future
in a little house up north,
that did not hold Ana,
or his records,
or their child,
new and clean
as a perfect
porcelain tub.

Why do the little ones run, he asks.
Why do they beam?
How do they write such simple poetry?

The bud is drawn more than the blossom.
Death is a bird, a vulture.
He told terrifying tales in every dialect,
as his cat pretended to be jealous.
While the floppy pup
learned to speak whiskey.

His lonely liver shouted existence into the night,
never breaking the cages that held us from epilepsy.
We were not ready.

The phone causes brain tumors
so we tune to the French Revolution
and pretend we have always been in love there.

I have always been poor

and America is an accident waiting to happen.

Always the coming catastrophe.
Always the shaking and
the high pitch of
modern literature.

"In the event of a major catastrophe ...
try and find me
because you're the type of person
that I'll be looking for".

6. *Mars in the Eighth*

Daily recitation

SOME OF THEM ARE SEARCHING
for a more creative way to say
they don't care.

Another clique.
Read their books,
sing their songs,
drink their alcohol,
mate.

I don't want to use another metaphor.
I don't want another symbol.

Motivating myself to live in many worlds at once.
Attempting to sound words with passion.

Where is that voice?
That single sound inclined to carry every forgotten
thing?

Words come out of me like a pot boiling over,
or I'm empty as slight wind through a cave.
I want Mary Daly to tell me my organs are not hollow
again.
I want her to remind me everyday.

Remind me that my hollowness could matter.

Tempted to denounce everything,
to never stand with or have discourse.

I'm meant to be in a city laying all on top of itself.
I'm meant to be stinging with the sounds and separateness.

Meant to be submerged in differences.
Fashioning myself to chaos
and pretending
it doesn't hurt to forget
we were married coming in,
we are married exiting.

Internalized texts that were ignored to begin with
so many writing themselves into history
at once
digging images of themselves up,

back
back
back

past the heavy cages and fabrics draped
so that there is little hope of a sprinting escape.

Perhaps I can drum up a larger vocabulary,
use another word fashioned for someone else's mouth.
Make another image that inevitably starves another person out.

Talk of trauma, talk of obsolescent movements.
The only conversation I'm really having is,
are they going to war with me?
When the serotonin runs out and they dust off father's whiskey?
Will you give up and send the anger horizontal?

Language was never ours.

I make maps in hesitant graphite
only to have them revised again and again.

A continent invaded by an accidental evening with a nationalist.

A trans woman bickers with a part of my mind when reading a neurology journal.

All the while Gaza cries in a darkness I made.
Turned the light off on them myself.

And I think they, whoever they are,
prefer my sadness.
A dull hope that can be easily extinguished
by an unedited polemic.

Killed the lord, left for the New World

THE QUESTION,
what will remain of us,
sends my insides on a tight jolt of terror.

The silence of my surroundings pacifies me.
The willingness of everyone around me
to remain content
with the warm porcelain
and the casual conversation.

I'll pretend. That this pursuit
for understanding,
that this social commentary in my hands
is worthy. Noble.

What will philosophy be
to a hungry civilization
settled upon barren soil?

I shudder at the thought
of blood and rape
totally consuming my home.

The fascist state
finally pulling it's sheepskin away
and demanding we provide
for its insatiable hunger.
The repression of my homeland
collapsing into its inevitable conquest,
once done discreetly abroad.

Can anyone in this silent town
hear my inner scream?

The woman sitting three feet away looks up
and glances a hello into my pin-sized pupils.
I force a slight smile.
I lie by omission.
I never say,
by 2059 Manhattan will be a starving island.

I never say:
Listen. Did you hear that?
two-hundred species just moaned in chorus
of untranslated languages
as they fell extinct.

Listen,
a tree is falling in a forest
surrounded by a crowd of men
deaf to their bargaining and begging.

A mountain is being gutted.

Listen,
the last of fifteen indigenous tribes
just called out to us
as they were being colonized ...

Finding the objective

I HOLD HER OFF,
tell her five stories
to keep her from the source
of my pain.
Before an audience
she suggests
the slow process of
carrying water from
reservoir to another
with a single bucket.

I've built a great desert
between our place of labor
and where I call home.

D. dreams of taking his horse through
the vast terrain and awakens with the notion
that he has no destination.

I hold her off away from my solitary evenings
where I stay up and write
in a cloud of smoke and
fill my pen with wine.

She wants to place her hands on where it hurts,
where cities and memories quake,
where I've built aquifers and dams
to contain and remain poised, elegant.
She could comb out the knots
in my aquatic garden bed
if there were time.

If there were not eleven pairs of eyes on our bodies
square with one another.
three chairs in a perfect triangle,
a shape with potential to produce
my life's works at once
given strategic prayer.

I am sitting with five women under my shirt.
I am sitting with their lives
and keeping their stories from exiting my throat.
L. gives all the proper answers
to ethical practice scenarios.
She vows before us to pass on her client.
To defer
in the event of an emergency.
I tear at the notion.
Saying that anybody
that lays out in front of me is a part of this crisis.

I am ludic,
anxious to make or advertise.

What of a dark night.
The guilt of death on your hands
staining her bright practice.

What of a woman
who has abandoned her body.

Refer, refer.

The revision of ego's script
and body bound in the cultural memory.

We tell the stories again and again
circling, circling
not arriving.

Until her hands are on my chest
until she believes she can hear a story of violation
and hold it
tenderly in her palms
with eyes unwavering
knowing that it is ours.
The women beneath my shirt
are kicking and hollering, finally.
Laying claim.
This is our objective,
a ground for movement.

There is not yet time
not yet space relinquished
from the bounds of
who or what is qualified
to know we share this burden.

I return to where I sleep
heart unwound a bit.
Still clinging tightly to the root of my discomfort.

D. tells me straight
that he is willing to love me,
willing to stand unguarded
where my life lies dormant.

He tells me like a surgeon prescribing
precise incisions and sutures
to our breathing addicts of pleasure.

We speak as if we are scheduling business.

His gift to me is his affection
which he says
is the source of his attachment.

I love him in my way.
I think I will read him like a novel
that I forget to take notes on.
Allowing scenes to visit
at some time when I am lonesome
and heavy with nostalgia.

He comes with a manual for love making.
He comes without romance
and the practical grunts of a working life.

I am that yearning impulse,
that myth of woman buried
in a Freudian Œdipal child's story.

I daydream of loving women
of loving in ways I've not explored.
I tell him I'll be writing my second thesis
on female anatomy.

And I feel like a stereotype
hands moving water in the kitchen sink,
arms shuttling laundry from the dryer to the bed.
Or I am a jukebox
sometimes wooing him with songs I sing,
or mysterious in constant study and scrawling.

In preparation

for my lovers,
curious women who defy institution
by choosing to honor their bodies.

In preparation
for my friends who boil over and into the streets
reclaiming their sex and sovereignty
over again.

They know everything has been done
and everything has been said
and so it must be displayed again.

Until that quantum leap,
the shining moment
of evolutionary theory showing blindingly through
some prophet's miracle.

I don't know what to make of this love
D. gives to me.
I still call it violence
and I cannot see beyond
the drink, the smoke,
the complacency.

His soul a departed ghost
that has yet to reinhabit his body.

I am alien here
where I plan to leave in two months' time.

Transient.

I hold off on making art

and stay with my old familiar writings.
I tell E. that I have found my clientele,
that I know where to touch
to move this ancient stagnation.

I've found my medicine.
A midwife,
located geographically and philosophically
in the time of my grandmother's failures.
Fingers on the pulse of a current
rippling out from seven prior generations.

Feminine sexuality

THEY WALK THE FOUR BLOCKS
to catch the last bus that runs down Market Street
at 11:08 p.m.

She reaches into her bag
retrieving a small book that
holds her bus pass betweens its pages.

"What are you reading?", he asks.
She passes it underhand to her right.
Feminine Sexuality, Lacan.

"Sexuality feminine,
why do you read
if you are woman?", he asks.

"Eh, he follows Freud", she says.
"He deconstructs the Œdipal myth".

"Oh", he says, looking at her.

"I have to go, this is my bus ...", she says.

Why does she read male theory of female sexuality
if she is female?

Rohini

IF THEY WERE TO DELIVER ME,
if I were made of them,
I would be
a dried-out wish bone
no one won a wish upon.

My secret thoughts were whispers,
small mantras I had taught myself
to repeat in bliss,
nameless, soundless,
the color of gold.

I thought,
I brought myself here,
I will escape on my own.

I hid a longing for a perfect witness.

In the event you arrive in a dark room
with a person convinced they are a stranger,
a sciatic snake that can not touch their own tail
you at least attempt a perfect union.

Sit back
and watch how it is done.

I have slipped into time and space
where intercourse is the proper narrative.

I do not consume shame or guilt any longer.
I have had my fill.

I am in abstinence,
born again and again,
virgin when the sun rises,
Shakti when I uncoil.

I am not confused of what I am
and damned to be misinterpreted.
The container restricts.

I dream the story of other lucidly,
knowingly suspended in illusion
of required assistance for deliverance.

I find one hand to clap
and the pleasure is mine.

Killing an old friend

THE CAFFEINE ELECTRICALLY
floods dreamworld from my morning body.
All that is not solid slips away fast.

I chase the glowing dimensions with my arms and fingers.
Swatting at a flock of crows with claws for palms.
It looks like a ritual dance at sunrise.

The worlds are gone from me.
I feel the presence of resonant memories in my body.
Those remaining, wrapped up inside
my organs, cabinets,
which hold blankets and trophies.

You are there,
a crystallized relic.
I can pull you out
and observe the antiquity of what we so alchemically forged.
Forged with ocean magic, sand, coal, fire, glass, tea leaves, and stone pillows.

The etchings are scrawled
questionable as drunken penbabble.

I do not recall this language.
I feel it in my body, sonar, a permeating presence.
It could swallow me if I let it unfold itself.

The walls of its mouth are made of murals.

Murals of forever-wet paint.
A splattering-smathering of rainbows
on someone else's sheets.

It speaks to the chaos in me.
To the little androgynous beach baby that played with
heat and salt.
A little grain of sand
that followed so many pedestrians home in their bathing
suit bottoms.

I like her very much.
Though I wish she would stop telling me about her pain
and confusion.
Her depth and tears have birthed new women.
She is far more fertile than she chooses to remember.

And you are with her.
A dæmon she liked to play with.
A dæmon that kept her safe.
Grabbing her by the hand when she ran into the street.

This orb has become fragile.
I can push it around with my breath, a soapy bubble.

And I want to destroy it.

I hold my finger out
and watch my new face reflected in its slick surface.
I nearly let it be for fear that you could die forever this
way.

My body sways like a pendulum,
in a trance my finger

juts out and, *pop!*

Our entheogenic memories
are gone.

On a few American writers

BENJAMIN WANTS TO WRITE
a stanza that will ferment into a chorus.

It was just three years ago
that he fell in love,
and when he said it aloud
I knew I could not doubt him.

There is no arguing with a smile,
as wide,
as drastically opposite
to boredom.
He wants to write a stanza
that will ferment into a chorus.

He scoffs at songs produced cleanly,
describing the making of pancake batter,
the tying of ribbons round doorknobs,
and hammocks spread between comfortably-spaced
trees.

We all sit on our bar stools,
asses going numb,
and wait upon that chorus.

A shot of Sapphire gin
each time we hear him sing Hallelujah.
Our livers dumbly wonder
if he will finally make a song of love
once he has fallen into sadness,

when he must sing as Orpheus
summoning a land goddess
past due for deep-sea diving.

David is a fallen angel.
He's changed his name nine times.

His present name is really perfect.
I won't write it here
because it might encourage him.

David wants to go to Switzerland
and if he cannot win the lottery then
he'll hang in a tree
or he'll live amongst northwestern trees.

He once loved a woman who loved him
more than his studies
then he decided he loved his studies
more than the both of them

and set off to bury himself in a stack of kitschy literature.

He rubbed the texts against his boyish skin,
decided he was wise,
and went to mix audio clips of western music
with flashing lights at wedding showers.

Those were years he spent with dust up to his elbows
digging through bins of vinyl he could afford.

He's a real philosopher
when he isn't a shaman.
When he is shaman

he invites the local girls to his tent
and plays doctor.
His business card boasts of headache cures.

He hasn't found the antidote for alcoholism.

He says, I heal them and they leave me,
so I'm up all night posing nude as a Greek statue
who's mysteriously discovered the promise of industrial-
ized kink.

I once attempted to transmit Oms and Ahs to him
through a telephone wire and live video stream.
Neither of us has found a substitute for old fashioned
skin on skin.

Something to do with rhesus monkeys and their
mothers ...
Maria is a pastel raindrop.
She wants her heart to show pink
through her summer dress
and she can't stop drawing with charcoal
in the mirror on her own chest.

She's mastered rings of chain smoke
and doesn't believe in cancer.
Even if you look her dead in the eyes
and repeat yourself several times.

If you asked her,
she'd tell you she's waiting to meet a true poet,
the ones from other continents
who lived long before the Internet.

Each month she's in love with a new one.
She keeps a blog called
Love Letters to Dead Men.

There are gangs
on every corner in her neighborhood
on damning campaign,
smearing Lorca, Neruda, Rumi or Rajneesh.
You might catch a sight of her
chasing yellowed pages down the block or
sulking back indoors at sunset
after a run in with rationalists.

Michael has it all figured out.
He doesn't write at all.
He's disposed of the word.
He dreams in Italian sepia
and the only sounds he makes
are sent through a tube amp.

We don't know if he's speaking jazz or sign language.

His art is the most like a tapestry
so someone is sure to buy him a Guinness
on the rare occasion he leaves the house.
And I am a writer who writes about writers writing.
I try to make a poem that won't read like a joke in the morning.

I only want a drink when there are exactly two quarters left in my wallet,
or when well-meaning persons want to cure me of my poverty.

Sabotage

PROMISE THAT YOU WILL HELP ME SABOTAGE THIS.
Not one more step,
until we both agree that this will end,
abrupt and half-hearted.

Would you be willing to kill a future for freedom?
Willing to plunge into the vulnerable depths which
supply our longing with fodder?

Our passions will blaze across this continent
with an intention to leave our countries barren,
clean, and new.

We would be left with tales of the old land
and a fear of re-creation.

Mourning long enough
to write our tragic trite memoirs
and grow bored of depression.

Finally choosing to synthesize a new
fertile reality.

7. *Sagittarius Rising*

06262015

YOU CAN BE YOUR OWN ANTITHESIS,
make what you don't want again and again.
You say you fear trusting
so you won't make it.
The world's a lonely place
when every friend's an asset
who's withholding something.
You take without asking
and respond entitled,
well, you should have stopped me.

You can be your own recurring dream
saying you want honesty.
Then hide from yourself
concealing all depth.
Only the persona breathes.

Left again by a friend
who thought you a stranger.
With lovers like you
who needs pimps, johns,
or bosses.
It's too late
socialization's taken fate.
Connection's a passing meal ticket
a dollar, an orgasm.
For the man who fears what he desires most,
ballads are carcasses of slack copper strings
beneath the scrawling of a poet's
hopeless dead language.

You can be your own antithesis
make what you don't want
again and again.

For one who's forgotten how to be a friend
trust and honesty are unknown values
inconvertible currency.

07162015

NO ONE WARNED ME YOU MUST SELL YOUR SOUL
to remain a poet beyond the twilight of youth.
Exchange conversation with grayness
for symbols that ring a different note
between each pair of ears.

When I was young I wrung syllables
from the morning and longing,
excavated verse from murk and ocean cliffs.
My tongue conjures memories of taste
for each passing desire or contraband.
I drift to sleep with a mind still as low tide shore
without footprints.

If a stanza happens to come to me while walking home
I advance into a sprint,
my keys chime and thud as they drop
upon the thin blue carpet of the doorway
and I fumble to grab a pen and paper
before the images drift away.

Sam forgets to take his meds
and weathers a few manic waves
to get the words flowing again.
He works himself up into filling a few notebooks
finally shuffling into the kitchen disheveled,
declaring, he's met Satan!
The people sitting 'round the table forget to blink.

I'm happy to be unconsumed by a life of art,
to not make situations of people or places,

to not need to document
a disappointment, a flutter of hope,
to not be self-consumed.

I've become content in being ordinary,
to only wonder when I will have time
to do my laundry one week next spring.
I don't sketch portraits
because it's too much to make models of people
and expect them to stand still,
too obnoxious to go dragging my fingers
across every dusty groove in someone's apartment,

to inquire about each freckle or scar.

I've made monuments and prophets
out of mundane and arbitrary people and things.
I've volumes of prose
they go unread,
they no longer speak.

First line

HAD HER HEART FOR A MOMENT
while you were weighing out the pros and cons,
calculating reciprocated desire.
The faucet ran and ran
until it rusted shut.

Waiting for a go-ahead.
Waiting for a friendly sign.

These days everything is irreverent
until someone takes a risk   ·
and says it's time.

Biting your lip,
holding your breath.
How does one tell when it's alright to
let down the first line?

That sweet woman
she keeps her heart tender
as twelve trains pass by
absent of her lover.

Who knows what finally sent her home ...
a change of clothes, of heart,
a final slump toward nihilism?

I don't believe in love.
I'm not sure why I write of it.
Everyone is trying still,
and so I document it.

Matt allows the decision to be made for him.
People come and go as they please
and if no one throws themselves at his feet,
he'll be lonely.
His heart's grown too old.
Dried out in a southwestern desert somewhere.
I am too unconcerned.
I have forgotten what to say.
I have learned to keep it loose and tight.

Waiting for a go ahead.
Waiting for a friendly sign.
Bite your lip, hold your breath.
Neither of us know when to let down the first line.

10192015

I HAVE LEARNED TO FEAR LESS THAN VIOLENCE.
I know the insidious nature of thick silence
that conceals depths of wishes
couples cast to secure their safety
their homes, their reputations.

I can disappear.
Evaporate like fleeting recollections of preference,
or slow erosion of opinion that shows faint
through worn fabric of a shallow life
that is torn through to arrive at emptiness.

I can will to starvation
and force each pleasure
back out of my stomach.
I can slip like whispers thin as ghosts
from room to room.
And fend off tears divined from
the only emotion I can sympathize with,
longing for a promise one took for granted,
promises given to children who have no filter,
no skepticism.

When the vulnerable become disappointed
they revoke their magic.
They go numb and hide in an artful shelter
of invisibility.
Common sadness no longer moves me.
I cry for those who recoil in fetal lonesome.
A static bitter permeates regress.
The remaining hues that show through

dense gray and black and white
are blue of steel guitar strings
or amber of subdued anger.

The soup is cold, it sits unconsumed,
as steam rises into a frozen sky
of new betrayal.

11222015i

WHEN I HARM YOU, I HARM MYSELF.
When I harm earth, I harm you.
When I harm an animal, I harm your mother.
When you harm earth, you harm my children.
I want you to feel my pain.
I want you to feel the sorrow of earth
and its animals, and its people.
And I want to be sorrowful with you.
I want us to become sullen, depressed
and then enraged.
I want for our anger to shake the people,
asleep with numbness, awake.
Because our hearts are breaking,
and even whispers of compassionate condolence
cause us to wince.
As the violence is all around us.
It has become the way we eat,
the way we speak,
the way we breathe.
It is how we walk.
I want you to mourn with me.
And I want us to fight together.
I want us to protect each other.
Because:
When I harm you, I harm myself.
When I harm earth, I harm you.

When I harm an animal, I harm your mother.
When you harm earth, you harm my children.

12082015i

I SAW US OLD.

He was moving slowly
toward a seat at a restaurant table.
I wanted to grab him by the elbows
to help him sit
as his legs were shaking
and his back was curved.
I turned away with impatient agony.

The woman with him smiled,
her content gaze
rested easeful into the lines of her face.
I thought she must have been fifteen years
younger than him.

What were they to one another.
He braving a Friday evening downtown.
Her, limber, luminous,
bearing no anxiety,
pacing slowly behind his every movement,
attentive, undisturbed.
Was she daughter, niece, lover, nurse, or cousin.

I observed them in ambiguous celebration.
And thought, one day we may be like this.

12082015ii

HE LAMENTED FEARING PSYCHOSIS.
To be taken by nature,
consumed by demonic constellation.
Neurons, synapses, transmitters
turning, moving into uncommon shapes.
Mind spinning, dropping like the mood
of a lysergic acid diethylamide midnight.
He fears what he is most curious of.
Poking, prodding, stroking the Westerner's great beast.
Uncertain of whether rapport has been maintained.
All those years:
rolling, rotating it, holding it,
straining it through his fingers,
rough sketches, wet paintings,
almost making love to it.

Mine comes like a golden smog.
A breath of sunset
that takes my stride,
observes my aloneness,
embraces my vision and body,
flooding my shadow,
making it all too warm,
too connected.

Madness strings the details of life together.
A silver thread collecting small colorful glass beads;
offering them in a strand.
Tempting me with synchronicity.

Coincidence, harmony, paranoia

slide on top of one another,
a lens of concentric circles,
through which the world is a rose-hued horror.

A toast to madness,
to anyone's preferred sin.
To the twelve p.m. whiskey,
to the borderline flood of rocking passion,
the ascetic starvation,
the waiting, the counting, the tapping.
Momentum for the sake of momentum,
the hermetically sealed prison we make of our lives,
the room, the market, the park, the highway.

A toast to the safety valve,
that lets it all in one drop at a time.

12082015iii

I BEGGED NOT TO
and dreamed of your ruddy skin.
A tapestry of inflammation,
of sunburn,
of pocked landmarks.
Your whiskey lips
and liver large,
a second bosom.

I begged not to and remembered
your thick blonde chest
against my cheek;
in the morning, with puppy sweet talk,
and promises of intricate letters
mapping the heart of things;
licked, stamped, and sent off
across three towns,
traveling your shore to my city.

The distance is tepid and serene.
I can speak across it
as if I were reciting prose.
And you can dictate to me
which lines are poetry
and which are stagnant deepities.

Full of gin and breaking the silence of my works.
Delivering them one after another after another after
another.

Our works are houses we hide inside of.

We covet each other's property.
Held up in some corner booth,
in some warmly lit bar,
blessed with privacy.
You were a Jim Harrison,
I was a no-name poet, not quite an Anaïs Nin.
Wondering what my work could mean.
Wondering what your heart could mean.

With hands deep in the chill of our separate sleep.
I have not called or answered, except in the ice of that dream.

Our movement swept until the floor boards coughed wood grain.
We are shallow pools of champagne and half-writ letters to synthetic saviors.

Entanglement

I'VE HELD BACK FROM WRITING OUT
the tumultuous churning waves
I've rode and been consumed by.

They would flow thick from my pen
and splotch upon the paper.
Perhaps it would be best
to paint a large canvas
with dark and heavy gray
or stand still and calm in a pitch black night
where there are no stars,

or allow tears to fall
and dry on a blank page.
Instead I walked about brimming with water,
and napped with a mind full of surreal threat.

I enjoy his world of possibility.
His apartment, his mind
a fun house of fleeting mirrors
that reflect the depth of things,
illuminating the places
where my brow tends to furrow.

He is a warm light
that I can hold my heart against.
I find my body easily remembers
how to harmonize with it.

I want to question the narrative,
the myth that plays me.

The wide brush I use to paint
over our masterpiece.

I am not certain.
My guts sense fear.
They have learned
to quickly detect defeat.

Perhaps the epiphany of his light heart,
my deep sorrowful passionate lust
and amorous landscape
are truly like oil and water,

truly an alchemical process
that cannot forge
some magnificent unknown alloy,
alliance.
I've been loved gently.
I've been touched by soft language
and a reassuring gaze.
I have demanded arm's length.

I am fooling myself with longing.
I could love him gently,
like a sister or cousin.
But his eyes are too kind.
I am startled by their wisdom
and feel inclined to climb
inside his gaze.

To huddle myself forever in his chest.
To breath in what he exhales.
To take his tongue in my mouth,
again and again.

My admiration quickly becomes lust.
I long to climb inside of him.
To lose myself in a humid dream,
where we are wild
and defiant of the world's puritanism.

Still, there is the heavy probability
that I am not for him in this way.
In any way.
And the question bores me,
for I long to live in the action of love.

A Cassette!?

ON THE SECOND NIGHT,
momentarily succumbing to intuition,
she thought,
I should not have shaved and trimmed for this.

In the morning,
she was certain
that he would be gone
before her hair grew out again.

She called him by her own name,
and he called her by his.

The love they learned to give themselves
was presented.
And once revealed

attempted concealment
of disappointment.

I miss your body next to mine

I MISS YOUR BODY NEXT TO MY BODY.
I woke this morning into a memory.
I turned to find your face and eyes.
My arm almost reached for you.
My dry fingers almost reached
for your warm hand.

My lips twitched and quivered
as they readied to give you a greeting kiss.
Two kisses, one for your cheek
and one for your mouth.

Two kisses
to say, hello,
welcome.

I would wonder if I could make love with you.
If you would let me run my tongue
along the skin of your chest and stomach.

I realized that you were not there.
I had woke into e. cummings' memory.
Some dead poet who knew love better than I.
I miss your body next to my body.

01122015

SCALES BLUNT OBJECTS USED TO STUN AND
paralyze dissidents.
You were both and all.
You were eight corners and vacant.
Our wounds were bare.

I promised not to put my hand in,
you promised not to touch it.
Don't touch it. Don't touch it.

It won't stop bleeding.
The wound is endless.

I've never felt this hideous,
this broken.
You were the perfect human.

We ate each other alive.

Sent new ghosts into other worlds
to play out the remainder of loves
we could not give.

I won't list preferred intoxicants.
I'll never tell them what you did.
Wine is the pleroma.

ABOUT THE AUTHOR

MAIA SPRING CARABAJAL is a poet, scholar, and musician currently living in Northern California. She began writing in her teens after being introduced to the Beat poets and Anne Sexton. Her early work was regularly featured in the anarchist art zine, *Pages Per Content*. Carabajal is presently completing dual degrees in psychology and philosophy at the University of California, Davis.

www.ingramcontent.com/pod-product-compliance
Lightning Source LLC
Chambersburg PA
CBHW030430010526
44118CB00011B/579